He sits at the table in a baggy Boston Red Sox sweatshirt, staring at the blank sheet of paper before him. A sound from outside makes him look up, but he forces himself to concentrate. He closes his eyes for a moment. Then he opens them and begins to write:

> I walked out side to find my self ingulfed in darkness then From the wood I see two Floating Green Gleeming eyes looming toward me side-By-side floating up and down Faster and faster then suddenly the Garage light plows over the Green eyes to reveal snarf my little cat Pleeding to Get in

The boy who wrote this is Joseph, a ten-year-old fourth grader who also happens to be our youngest son. As we worked on *Teaching the Qualities of Writing* (TQW), we tried to keep Joseph in mind, along with the millions of novice young writers like him in classrooms reflecting diverse languages and cultural backgrounds.

Look back at what Joseph wrote. Surely there are limits to citing your child's writing as an example, but in this case it serves a useful purpose. We admire the rich vocabulary while, as parents, we cringe at the spelling errors, the fragments, the words that should be capitalized. Like most young writers Joseph has distinct strengths and weaknesses that don't cancel one another out.

It's helpful to remember that learning to write, like learning any complex skill, develops over a period of years. Students have already begun the process before they enter your classroom at the start of a new school year; they will continue it long after they leave. You only join them for a stretch of their journey. At best you bring to your teaching a perspective and language consistent with the teachers they have already had and those they have yet to meet.

We should also remember that writing is not a single skill but a bundle of skills, including encoding meaning, organizing ideas, using details, rereading, revising, using correct spelling and punctuation, etc. Although it may appear that learning to write requires teaching hundreds of things, it's useful to consider discrete skills within a larger framework, which we call the *Qualities of Writing*.

We have committed our professional lives to helping teachers find wiser ways of teaching writing. It is our fervent hope that TQW helps promote our major passion—nurturing teachers and the young writers with whom they work.

JoAnn Portalupi   Ralph Fletcher

Teaching
The Qualities
of Writing

JoAnn Portalupi and Ralph Fletcher

Photography: Deb Bohne and David Stirling

The authors and publisher wish to thank those who have
generously given permission to reprint borrowed material.

Library of Congress Catalog-in-Publication Data
CIP data on file with the Library of Congress
ISBN 0–325-00629-6

Printed in
the United States of America
on acid-free paper

08 07 06 05 04 VG 1 2 3 4 5

*first*hand
An imprint of Heinemann
A division of Reed Elsevier Inc.
361 Hanover Street
Portsmouth, NH 03801-3912
www.heinemann.com
Office and agents throughout the world

Teaching The Qualities of Writing: Teacher's Guide

I Understanding the Qualities of Writing

*Writing works well when it is strong in
ideas, design, language, and presentation
and infused with voice.*

IDEAS

The writer must have something to say. Strong writing conveys rich, plentiful ideas that are developed in engaging, even surprising ways. The writer understands his relationship to the ideas and delivers them with confidence to the reader.

DESIGN

Helter-skelter ideas, no matter how interesting, won't cut it. In the hands of a skillful writer, ideas are presented in an orderly fashion. Strong writing has shape, architecture, and an overall design. The writer makes critical decisions about how the ideas relate to one another. What matters most? Paying attention to design, the writer hones the ideas until they are organized into a seamless whole. Sound writing has a cohesion that suits the writer's purpose.

LANGUAGE

The language a writer chooses directly affects how we experience the ideas found on the page. In a strong piece of writing, the language allows ideas to take flight. The skilled writer understands the nuances of language, how one word can make a difference, and how the cadence of sentences contributes to the music readers will hear.

PRESENTATION

After all the hard work, a writer hopes to be read. Every possible barrier that stands between the writer and the reader—messy handwriting, incorrect spelling, and disorderly papers—has to be removed. Successful writing respects the reader's need for clean, correct presentation. Maybe Nancie Atwell put it best: "Good writing needs what readers' eyes expect."

Underlying Core Beliefs

Three core beliefs lie at the heart of TQW:

1. Young Writers Need Frequent Time to Write

The wisdom on learning to write has shifted. When we were students, our teachers spent more time instructing us on writing than we spent actually writing. We know today that kids develop as writers when given a steady diet of writing time enhanced by fewer minutes spent on teacher instruction. We believe students need sustained time (25—35 minute writing stretches three to five times a week) when they can deeply engage in the act of writing.

TQW embraces the paradox of education: the teacher can teach ideas, but they must be implemented by the student, when that student is ready and in that student's particular way. Lots of time spent writing gives them ample opportunity to experiment and put to work the techniques we offer them.

While there is no one way to teach writing, we believe that a writing workshop creates the conditions under which students can experience the real pleasures and challenges of writing. The writing workshop environment features student choice, sustained writing time, mechanics taught in context, and careful response during regular writing conferences. Teacher instruction occurs during whole-class or small-group minilessons and within individual writing conferences. We know of no better structure for growing competent writers. (See our *Writing Workshop: The Essential Guide* Heinemann, 2001, for detailed ideas on running a workshop.)

2. Writers Need to Be Readers

Learning to write progresses hand-in-hand with learning to read. We don't mean learning to decode and comprehend meaning. Rather, we're talking about an aesthetic kind of reading with an awareness that the words have been deliberately chosen by another writer. To encourage that kind of reading, most TQW lessons:

- *Provide a powerful exemplar text that students can use as a model.*
- *Point out an accessible strategy or technique the author used.*
- *Encourage students to try the strategy in their own writing and show them exactly how they might do so.*

These lessons rely on a "close encounter with a text." We want students to cozy up to texts they can learn from, to pull in for a front-row look at what the writer has done and how she did it. A teacher recently said to us: "Literature-based minilessons first impacted my students' writing by giving them another voice to listen to, another 'teacher.'" Teaching is such a lonely profession. It's intriguing to think of these model texts as co-teachers in the classroom.

Ultimately we want students to develop the habit of "reading as a writer," to consciously pick up a text with this question in mind: What can I learn from this writer? Students will apply this skill to their own writing as they read and ask themselves: How can I make this writing the best it can be?

3. Talk Is a Crucial Ingredient in Writing Classrooms

If we had to identify one factor that marks classrooms that produce strong writing and confident writers, it would be *quality conversation*. In these classrooms students and teachers read and talk about books in very specific ways. They develop a language that ultimately gives students insight into how to incorporate the elements of good writing into their own work.

We expect the lessons in TQW to work as catalysts for real conversation about the writerly craft. That's our goal—to get your class humming with rich talk about writing. This won't be limited to teacher-to-student talk; it will also include student-to-teacher and student-to-student dialogue. You will want to create "white spaces" that invite student conversation. Look for these spaces during the lessons as well as during writing conferences and discussions following read-alouds.

A Word About How Students Internalize the Qualities of Writing

For every writing technique or strategy you teach, students will go through a natural process of internalizing it. As you work with these lessons, be aware that students will fall at different points along this continuum:

- *I hear about it.*

- *I see it when you point it out.*

- *I can recognize it myself in someone else's work and appreciate it.*

- *I can try it on my own.*

- *I can use it successfully.*

It's much easier for students to notice a particular technique a writer uses than to use that technique effectively in their own writing. Expect that. Don't measure a lesson's success by whether or not a student immediately puts it to use effectively. There is usually a time lag that varies from writer to writer. Students may carry the tool of a new technique around for a long time before they grasp it and put it to use in their own work. Let's call this "sink time," the time a student needs for the idea to settle deep into the consciousness.

An idea put forth in a single minilesson will be nurtured as students work with it outside the boundaries of that day's work. Every time they come in contact with a text (during a new TQW lesson, during a read-aloud, or as they listen and respond during peer writing conferences), students have an opportunity to explore the qualities you have presented in earlier lessons. As your class continues to write, read, and talk together, students will develop a more sophisticated understanding of the Qualities of Writing and use this enhanced knowledge as they read and revise their own writing.

The Qualities
Up Close and Personal

*The graphic to the left suggests
a way to conceive of the four qualities.*

Writer

IDEAS

DESIGN

LANGUAGE

PRESENTATION

Reader

The writer's attention shifts from writer (what I have to say) to the reader (what the *reader* needs to hear). Note that ideas inhabit the widest part of the V, since the writer casts a wide net to pull in necessary ideas, facts, and information. Presentation resides at the narrowest part of the V, because at this point the writer's focus is line-by-line, word-by-word. Although we are going to explore these elements separately, it's important that we don't teach them as isolated stages that always happen in this order—ideas, design, language, presentation.

A skilled writer has all these concerns in mind at any given time and understands the connections among them. The spotlight shifts throughout the process, shining more brightly at times on one quality or another. Writers deal with each of these elements every time they complete a piece of writing, but the whole is always greater than the sum of the parts. Still, there is a rough sequence to the process of writing. Most writers dive into ideas before grappling with design. Once they have some kind of plan or focus for these ideas, they can attend more closely to the language used to present them (though sometimes the idea may be sparked by a fragment of language). As they move closer toward finishing and preparing to have the writing read, the appearance and correctness of the writing fall under the spotlight.

There's another significant reason we showcase these writing qualities in a V—it stands for voice and reminds us that voice is not a separate quality but a common thread that infuses all four qualities. Voice manifests itself in the kinds of ideas the writer chooses to put forward, how he decides to organize them, and in the particular way this writer's work appears on the page. The most tangible evidence of voice can be found in language; a writer's language conveys the rhythms, quirks, and cadences of a real person speaking to us through written words. Although we don't have a separate quality for voice, we have identified two dozen "voice lessons" each of which suggests a way to recognize, create, or strengthen voice in writing. Look for the *voice* tag in the upper right-hand corner of these lessons.

Let's explore each Quality of Writing in greater detail:

IDEAS

DESIGN

LANGUAGE

PRESENTATION

VOICE

A young writer sits down to work. The blank page stares back at her. Poised above the paper, she thinks… After a few minutes the pencil begins moving across the page. One idea at a time, she builds the story. Or maybe she's writing a report on a favorite animal and thinks, What do I know about raccoons? Again, idea by idea, brick by brick, she builds her report. At its most basic, writing relies on the writer's ability to generate ideas. Even before a writer thinks of shaping, ordering, or detailing those ideas, she has to gather them in her mind.

Don Murray reminds us, "Good writing starts with honest, specific, accurate information." Skilled writers can bring the insider perspective to any topic, even if it is outside their experience. They convince us with the quality of their ideas. But with beginning writers, drawing on an actual experience (event, person, hobby, etc.) gives them a place in their mind to return to when generating ideas.

Strong writing requires an abundance of ideas. But that doesn't mean skilled writers use every idea they dream up. In the long run we need to help students learn about the quality of ideas—to recognize which ideas, out of the many they generate, will best serve them when they write.

For a list of Ideas lessons, see page 100.

The Ideas lessons fall into five sub-qualities:

TOPICS

We all know the magic that results when a student encounters a "just right" book. A similar magic happens when a young writer finds a topic that's just right, one with which he has enough experience to offer inside information, ideas, and insight when writing about it. That's why personal narrative is usually a good place to start for young writers. In TQW we embrace the concept of student choice, believing that the best, truest topics lie deep within each of us. But where does a student find a good idea for writing, and once she has found it, how does she bring it alive? Most students find it natural to write from experience; others may flounder in the "vacuum of choice" and need our help.

DETAILS

The devil's in the details, the old saying goes. These specifics are the vehicles writers use to flesh out their ideas. Even a single well-chosen detail can go a long way toward bringing alive a piece of writing. Writers can draw details from the internal world (thoughts, feelings) as well as the external world (actions, observations, sensory details). Often a student has a wealth of ideas in his head, but these ideas never make it onto the page. Student writers need to learn how to generate lots of details, recognize the best ones, and use those details to strengthen the writing.

COMPARE/CONTRAST

One of the best ways to explain an idea is by comparing it with, or showing it in relation to another. This skill is simpler to explain than it is to execute, but it can be applied across genres—in poetry, narrative, and especially in nonfiction when the student has to explain a big new idea.

CHARACTER/SETTING

In beloved books like *Maniac McGee* and *Harry Potter,* the characters seem to walk into our lives, full-blown and alive. Creating believable characters is much harder for young writers, especially students who seem far more interested in driving their plots full speed ahead. We can give them a number of concrete ways to bring alive their characters and the settings in which they live and act. Attending to character and setting encourages students to slow down and write deeper, richer stories. The lessons in this section also help students strengthen their nonfiction writing, particularly biography.

POINT OF VIEW

Telling a story in the first person (*I*) is the most natural way to write, but it's not the only option available to the writer. TQW offers lessons to introduce the three main points of view: first person (*I*), second person (*you*), and third person (*he/she/they*). Each new point of view gives the writer more options for revealing the story to the reader. As in all TQW lessons, we draw on models that will be familiar to many students.

IDEAS

DESIGN

LANGUAGE

PRESENTATION

Have you ever walked into a store, flea market, or garage sale crammed with fascinating items that are jumbled together in such a disorganized manner you can't find what you're looking for? If you're lucky, you stumble onto something valuable, but you spend most of the time feeling frustrated and lost. This description applies to writing that is rich in ideas but lacking in design. Well-designed writing conveys the comforting sense that the writer is taking us (the reader) by the hand and leading us on a well-paced tour of her "store" of ideas.

Many students at this age find this quality a challenging one. A kid's thought, talk, and writing often follow a peculiar organization that makes sense only to that student. And while it is always tempting to impose our design on students' writing, it's important to recognize that design is another important, personal decision each young writer must make, a decision that can amplify the voice of that writer. Every writer has to wrestle with the question, How can I best arrange my writing so that it makes sense to me and will also make sense to a reader?

For a list of Design lessons, see page 100.

The Design lessons in TQW contain six sub-qualities:

ORGANIZATION Organization isn't something to think about during prewriting and then forget about. The writer must also think about this quality while drafting and while revising for meaning. Some young writers have an innate sense that writing should have a beginning, a middle, and an end, but others do not. And even those who do need exposure to other ways they might organize a piece of writing. One of our long-term goals is helping students respond more flexibly in this regard. The idea is not to impose an organizational schema arbitrarily but rather to find the right organization for that particular piece of writing.

FOCUS Everyone has trouble with this one, whether it's an adult looking at a restaurant menu or a child told he might choose one thing in a toy store. For every piece of writing, the writer must ask, what is my angle on this topic? Focus involves selecting, choosing a slice, narrowing a big topic (*school*) to something manageable (*late lunch*). We need to teach children how to use a thematic focus to select ideas that fit a central theme. TQW gives students powerful models and lots of hands-on practice to make them aware of all the different ways writers focus and why it is so important. Attending to this issue brings another unexpected benefit: sharpening the focus in a piece of writing almost always sharpens the voice.

BEGINNINGS A strong lead sends an immediate signal to the reader: *I am thinking about you. I am working hard to keep you engaged.* As we raise this issue with students, we need to demystify it by giving them models that show alternative ways of beginning a piece of writing. A good lead often does more than simply hook the reader; it can also introduce the pattern or design for the rest of the writing.

ENDINGS Readers love to be hooked but also crave satisfying closure. (How many times does a bad ending ruin an otherwise good visit, meal, movie, or book?) This desire for a strong ending cuts across genres and is true in fiction, nonfiction, and poetry. We break down this big idea by providing a number of lessons that show students various ways they can end a piece of writing. Students may never have considered that there are as many different kinds of endings as there are leads.

TIME Time presents young writers with both a challenge and another way to organize their writing. Inexperienced writers are often controlled by time—laying out their stories chronologically. More experienced writers learn that time (pacing, slowing down here, speeding up there) is just one more element to control.

SHAPE Every story has its own shape, some more distinctive than others. We can help students recognize the circular shape of *The Wizard of Oz* and get a feel for other story shapes. Recognizing story shape is a design skill that requires students to move from the concrete *what* of the story (what it's about) to the *how* (how it is shaped). With time students will begin applying what they know about story shape to their own writing.

IDEAS

DESIGN

LANGUAGE

PRESENTATION

An artist may work in oil, pastel, or watercolor. Language is the medium a writer uses to "paint her prose." Like any craftsperson, the writer respects the material, savoring the heft of a particular word or phrase, taking satisfaction in the way one sentence snaps together with the next one. Acquiring more skillful ways of using written language is part of the process we go through our entire lives as we absorb new words and meanings and syntaxes. The goal is to better communicate what we want to say.

When it comes to language, students' growth will not be a straight upward-pointing graph. Students cannot stretch their language without a great deal of experimentation, trying new words, new constructions, etc. We need to remember to affirm their attempts, even when the initial results are not stellar.

For a list of Language lessons, see page 101.

Five sub-qualities help define the quality of Language:

CLARITY

In his book *On Writing Well*, William Zinsser extols the virtues of the simple, clear sentence. Writing clear prose requires the writer to stand back and recognize excess verbiage, and be willing to cut it, however painful that might be.

WORD CHOICE

This is a blood relative (or at least a neighbor) of clarity. The writer chooses the right word to deliver what he wants to say. Using a general word ("Grandma gives me stuff") leaves the reader with only a vague image. Using the wrong word ("Grandma gives me antiques") communicates erroneous information.

Our long-range goal is for students to have sufficient vocabulary at their fingertips to communicate a rich range of ideas. Until that happens, we can acknowledge that they know a limited number of words. In this case, we can show them tools to use (a thesaurus, for instance) to gather a wider range from which to choose. We want to develop in our students not merely a bigger vocabulary but also the ability to choose the word that says exactly what they mean.

SENTENCES

Variety is the spice of life. Whoever first said this might have been a teacher, or certainly a reader. Children at this age use all kinds of syntax when they speak. But when their thoughts get channeled into written form, they often turn out sentences that have a sameness about them. We don't want to read sentences of the same length and pattern over and over again. It's important to show students how they can play with the "clay" of their sentences by beginning them in different ways or combining shorter ones. Of course, gaining this kind of mastery will come easier for some young writers than for others.

MUSIC

Music has everything to do with how writing sounds to the reader's ear. Sound is influenced by the choice of individual words as well as the cadence with which words move from one to another. Alas, the sentences written by many students (and a lot of adults for that matter) could better be described as more *serviceable* than musical. These sentences get the reader from point A to point B, and that's about it. We can teach students a number of strategies (onomatopoeia, alliteration, repetition) they can use to create sentences that will be pleasing to the reader's ear.

VOICE

Written language is supremely personal in that it reflects the person writing it. When we speak of voice, we mean "personality-on-paper," the sense that these words have been written by a flesh-and-blood person with all the quirks, passions, and failings of any other person. Writing that has voice makes us want to keep reading. Not only that, it makes us care about the person behind the words. We need to teach voice not as some exalted writing state but as a natural element. Voice is present in everything we write. Once our students can recognize this quality in their own and others' work, they can learn how to strengthen it.

IDEAS

DESIGN

LANGUAGE

PRESENTATION

Nasdijj, a Navajo writer, says, "Still, I know nothing about the technical stuff, like where to put a comma... What I know about writing has to do with where to put your heart." Nasdijj is right: it *is* important to know where to put your heart. But in the end, the comma needs to be put in the right place, because placing it there ensures that the reader will receive the heart of your words.

If you lay out a time-line for a single piece of writing, you'll notice that the writer leaves the work just as the reader picks it up. The quality of presentation stands at the crossroads between writer and reader. Where earlier the writer's attention has been on meaning and how best to convey it, now the writer wishes to clear the way for the writing to be read. The quality of presentation includes all those things that invite readers to pick up a text and enable them to read it with ease.

Presentation is akin to "curb appeal" in real estate. The house with curb appeal attracts more potential buyers eager to take a look. During the publishing process, a writer decides how she will present her writing to the reading public. Writing that has been published with care invites readers to pick it up. The quality of presentation includes all those things that make writing "reader friendly": the surface features of print (punctuation, spelling) and the syntactical features of language (subject-verb agreement). When the rules of grammar and mechanics are in place, there's a transparency to the words and sentences that allow the other qualities to shine through.

For a list of Presentation lessons, see page 101.

The Presentation lessons fall into four sub-qualities:

CONVENTIONS In too many classrooms the teaching of mechanics and conventions has been isolated from real writing. When this happens, students get the mistaken idea that "creative writing" and "skills" don't mix. We believe that writing instruction must include the teaching of conventions (fragments, run-ons, paragraphing, etc.) and that these skills become most sensible when taught in the context of each student's writing. For students who are making the transition to English from their native language, there will be a wider range of grammar-related issues to address. While we do not lay out a course of study for these students, we hope you will borrow from the ideas of how to work with students on sentence-level editing and use them to meet the specific needs of your students.

COOL TOOLS There is a new interest in teaching grammar and mechanics not as the "grammar police" but as tools that give writers increased range and flexibility (for example see *Image Grammar*, by Harry Noden, Heinemann, 1999.). TQW's "Cool Tools" section has been written in this spirit, not as "memorize this rule for the dash" but rather as "look what amazing things you can do with the dash."

EDITING The typical classroom energy dynamic is often "high teacher, low student." One way to change that is to expect students to be their own first editors. While we won't give students total responsibility for checking correctness in writing (we still act as "editor-in-chief"), we know students learn as they cast an editor's eye on their own work. TQW lessons help students get to know their own bad tendencies and become more skilled at proofreading their work.

FINAL FORM These lessons deal with publishing: how to choose what to publish and exactly how to make the writing look the way you want it to. They also ask the student to think expansively: What is my purpose in this writing? Who do I want to read this? What look do I want this to have? Form follows function, and if your students write for a variety of purposes (and we hope they do!), the writing will take many different forms: books, booklets, brochures, letters, bulletin boards, newspapers, photo albums, and science fairs. The TQW lessons help students bring more attention to publishing their work so they can take pride in delivering it to readers.

II How to Use TQW

We began writing TQW with a goal to present ready-to-use curriculum materials that teachers would find pertinent to the particular students in their classrooms. We hoped that we might write "smart" curriculum materials in the way the computer industry applies the term, materials that could be tailored to the idiosyncratic needs of a particular teacher. We envisioned materials that maintained the integrity of the teacher, that honored the central role she plays as she makes continual decisions about what and how to teach. At the same time we wanted to create materials that teachers could use with students in a hands-on way and, at the same time, develop the professional's knowledge about how to teach writing.

Just as no two students are alike, teachers also vary in their knowledge, level of comfort, and passion for teaching writing. Work settings differ as do curriculum and time demands. It would be foolish of us to think that all teachers need the same thing out of these program materials. Consequently, this is not a one-size-fits-all set of curriculum materials.

What's Inside TQW?

Materials that help you provide the instruction students need to improve the quality of their writing and develop your ability to read and diagnose your students' writing include:

- *112 TQW lessons*
- *Exemplar texts that serve as teaching models*
- *A plan for using the lessons by cycles*
- *A plan for using the lessons based on students' and teachers' needs and interests*
- *Looking-at-Student-Writing CD-ROM*
- *Instructional Challenge Chart*
- *Guidelines for English Language Learners*
- *The Writer's Lifeblood*
- *Publishing Possibilities*
- *Children's Literature Bibliography*
- *A Blank Road Map and four other Possible Yearly Road Maps*
- *Assessment and Record-keeping Forms*
- *Lesson Lists (by Quality and by Cycle)*

Looking-at-Student-Writing CD-ROM

The CD-ROM features three resources:

1. Authors Videos

Click on one of the five video titles and you'll see a clip of the two of us introducing TQW. We provide a little background information about who we are and why we believe that learning about the four Qualities of Writing, infused with voice, will help your students become more effective writers.

The five video clips are entitled:

- *Meet JoAnn Portalupi and Ralph Fletcher*
- *Understand the Four Qualities of Writing (infused with Voice)*
- *Learn How to Use the TQW Lessons*
- *Link Assessment to Instruction: the Looking-at-Student-Writing CD*
- *Support and Enjoy Your Student Writers*

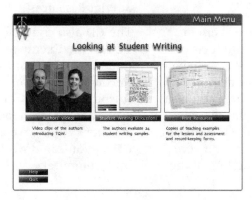

2. The Student Writing Discussions

On the Discussion List screen, you may select, by clicking on it, one of the 24 pieces of writing that are listed by student name, genre, grade, and length of discussion.

Then you go to the Discussion screen for that particular student. Here you have several options:

- *Print Student Sample* – make a printout of the student piece in case you want to share it with colleagues or other students. Perhaps you might try your hand at evaluating the piece yourself before listening to our discussion.

- *Hear Authors Read Sample* – listen to us read the students' writing and get a feel for our interpretation of it.

- *Hear Authors' Discussion* – listen to us discuss the pieces and see highlights on the student work that help you focus on the discussion.

- *Print Authors' Discussion* – print a transcript of our discussion.

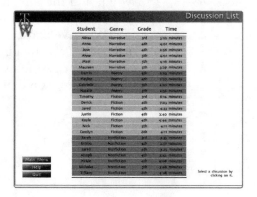

This section is a professional development course of study that's optional. In other words, you don't need to watch and listen to our discussion of individual student's writing in order to know how to use TQW.

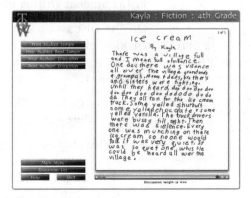

Nevertheless, we strongly recommend that you make time for it. The most effective teaching is responsive. We achieve the art of teaching when we are able to respond in sensitive, supportive ways to our students' specific needs and challenges. And we respond best when we really know our students—knowledge that we develop as we listen to them, talk with them, watch them in action in our classrooms, and analyze the products of their learning—in this case, their writing. We do hope you'll find the time to sit with us while we discuss 24 pieces of writing from students in grades three through six. We have chosen student writing samples that we believe reflect the kind of writing you will encounter in your own classrooms. As you listen to us and observe the samples, you'll broaden your understanding of the

Qualities of Writing and the ways in which they shape writing and the teaching of writing. You'll see how we discuss each developing writer and analyze

- *the student' strengths in the writing and*

- *one or two areas where the student needs work.*

What's more, if you look at the Instructional Challenge Chart (pages 41–43), you'll find specific TQW lessons that provide targeted support for specific needs such as the ones highlighted on the CD.

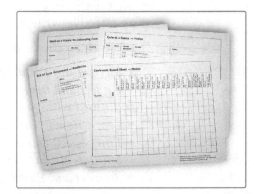

3. Print Resources

The CD also contains all the print resources that support TQW - the Exemplars (text and teaching guidelines you find on the back of the lesson cards), Assessment and Record-keeping forms, and the Writer's Lifeblood (inspiring quotes from insightful writers). While these are available in a ready-to-photocopy format in this Teacher's Guide, we also make them available on the CD so you can download and print them from your own computer.

You are the Professional Decision Maker

As the teacher you are the person best situated to make instructional decisions for your students.

This sentence conveys our fundamental belief about teaching. Making these decisions requires knowledgeable teachers who:

- *understand curriculum,*

- *know how to watch students at work, and*

- *plan instruction based on these observations.*

How you decide to order and arrange the lessons will be up to you, although we will offer several options to guide you in your decision-making. Ultimately we believe that once you begin working with these materials, you will find yourself selecting lessons based on the needs of your students. That means what you select to teach and the order in which you teach it will vary year to year, depending on the students you have and the curriculum you are working with.

Remember, you cannot possibly teach all of this in one year. Learning to write is a long-term voyage. You will join your students for one year (possibly two) of this journey. Your students will grapple with ideas, design, language, and presentation when they write for the first time in September. They will be dealing with the same qualities in May or June. What might you realistically hope to achieve during the course of one school year? You'll be aiming to:

- *develop students' abilities to think about the ideas they wish to convey.*

- *develop students' abilities to order/design their ideas.*

- *attune your students' ears to the sounds of language and the power of words to convey ideas and forge a connection with the reader.*

- *develop in your students the presentation skills (punctuation, spelling, mechanics) necessary to allow their writing to speak clearly to their audience.*

Let's first talk about the lessons themselves; then we'll look at the variety of ways you may choose to use them.

I write for two hours a day, but it's what I do for the other twenty-two hours that allows me to do that writing.

Don Murray

Getting to Know
the Lessons

*Each of TQW's
112 lessons follows
the same basic format:*

Thinking Point

Here's a brief introduction about the strategy being taught and how it fits with the kind of writing students at this age typically write.

Teaching Point

We believe that learning flows through language. In this spirit, we share carefully crafted language you can use to talk to students about specific techniques that can help them become stronger writers. Use the language we provide to teach these techniques until you feel comfortable with your own ways of talking about them. We urge you to "put your own fingerprints" on these lessons at any time, to tailor them until they feel and sound like you.

Prep Point

The Prep Point in each lesson lists the materials you and your students will need. The first item listed (and marked with a ◑) tells you what exemplar texts, organizers, and other resources appear on the back of each lesson card. These directly support the lesson and are designed, for the most part, to be viewed by students. Shorter texts may be recopied on the chalkboard or a chart or made into transparencies for group work. Longer texts work better as transparencies or handouts, one for each student. Except where necessary to the success of the lesson, we have left the presentation choice up to you.

The ◑ icon used in the Prep Point to identify material on the back of the card also appears at the point in the lesson where this material is used.

IDEAS / organization
DESIGN–◑ **FOCUS**
LANGUAGE / beginnings
PRESENTATION / endings
/ time
/ shape

Use a T

● **THINKING** Focus is
crucial. A
student who
finds her own slant/angle will
be able to write with voice.
Identifying a theme can be a
way to focus writing.

PREP
point

◑ "My Sister's Silly
Questions"

● **TEACHING** We're
find th
writin
much easier to write w
alive and sound like yo

Let's look at a piece of
This is a character sket

◑ Read "My Sister's Silly

Let's talk about Nicole's

Discuss.

Nicole's piece has hum
She could have written
clothes she wears, TV p
foods, etc. Instead, she
sister—her silly questio
questions are the "then
fair to say that she pick
revealed a lot about he

ematic Focus

...to be thinking about how to ...t focus for what you're ...ding the right focus makes it ...ice, to make the writing come

...g by Nicole, a fourth grader. ...her little sister.

...ions" aloud.

... What did she do well?

...ice, and interesting dialogue. ...out her little sister—what ...ms she watches, favorite ...d one thing about the little ...nd focused on that. Those ... main idea of the story. It's ...se questions because they ...r.

Notice that Nicole's story isn't a series of events you'd find in a story. It's more of a character sketch. A thematic focus like this (when you focus on one idea) works well if you're writing a character sketch instead of an actual story.

Today when you write, and whenever you write, get in the habit of asking yourself, What angle do I want to take? What's my focus going to be? Once you figure that out, you need to try to keep your writing focused on that.

FOLLOW UP point *Birthday Presents,* by Cynthia Rylant, is a fine picture book to model thematic focus.

This lesson is part of a series of lessons on "Focus." But it would also fit nicely in a study of how to bring character alive in writing.

Conference Questions:

What angle will you take on this topic?

What will your focus be?

Reference Key

In your portfolio you'll find the lesson cards organized by the four qualities of writing. In the upper right-hand corner of each card you'll notice an identification tag. The letter refers to the Quality the lesson deals with: I for Ideas, D for Design, L for Language, and P for Presentation. D-15 means that it is the fifteenth lesson found in the Design section. Note: this number is for identification purposes only, to help you find and retrieve the lesson cards. It does not refer to the sequence in which the lessons will be taught. Additionally, we identify the thirteen Launch cards so you can easily find and keep them organized as needed. Plus, in the upper right-hand corner, we also tag the lessons that showcase the element of "voice" in writing.

Follow Up Point

This section suggests ways you can extend the idea being taught and keep it alive for your students. You will also find realistic advice on what results to expect from teaching it.

Conference Questions

Here we suggest questions that help you bring the strategy from the lesson into your conferences with students. We believe that young writers need careful response to their writing. This typically occurs during the one-on-one writing conference, though at times you may decide to gather a small group of students to confer with. Writing conferences are the centerpiece of the writing workshop. There truly is an art to conferring well with students and we don't attempt to teach that here. But these Conference Questions will suggest a way to start. (For more information, look at our chapter on conferring in *Writing Workshop: The Essential Guide,* Heinemann, 2001.)

Getting Started:
The Launch Cycle

Peter Elbow reminds us that a writing teacher should be both a "good host and a good bouncer." We designed the Launch Cycle keeping in mind that being a good host is crucially important early in the year. We need to give students an early signal that they can write for us. The six-week Launch Cycle features a predetermined order of lessons to introduce you and your students to writing and help create the sense of community necessary to nurture their growth. The Launch Cycle offers students a chance to begin working within each of the four qualities while stressing the more important goal of developing in them an eagerness to keep writing. By the end of this six-week cycle, your students will have a notion of how writers find topics and will have taken several of their own pieces to final form. If you've

built in time for sharing, they will understand the value of giving and receiving response. They are now ready for new challenges—information and strategies that will help them improve the quality of their writing.

Since you'll probably kick off the school year with this cycle, our main intent is to make students comfortable with writing. Instead of having students writing in the first week, you may decide to read aloud picture books that invite them to start telling their own stories.

You'll find the thirteen Launch lessons, shrink-wrapped and tabbed *Launch* in the front of the TQW portfolio.

Launch Cycle

● *WEEK ONE*
φ I-4 **Dig Up Buried Stories**

● *WEEK TWO*
φ I-1 **Create an Authority List**

φ I-12 **Free-Write for Specifics**

● *WEEK THREE*
φ D-30 **Find Your Focus**

φ I-17 **Use Supporting Details**

● *WEEK FOUR*
φ D-15 **Use a Thematic Focus**

φ D-16 **Use a Time Focus**

● *WEEK FIVE*
φ L-23 **Use Verbs That Describe Action**

φ L-22 **Use Precise Nouns**

φ L-21 **Use Choice Adjectives**

● *WEEK SIX*
φ P-10 **Edit with a Checklist**

φ P-8 **Be Aware of Words You Commonly Misspell**

φ P-11 **Fix Spelling Errors**

Building Community During the Launch Cycle

You can teach all the nifty lessons in the world, but without certain intangibles such as community and a safe environment that encourages risk-taking, your students will not grow into strong, confident writers. Here are some ideas for creating community in your writing workshop.

We suggest you use these ideas during the Launch Cycle; however, please feel free to choose the ones you like and use them when it seems best for your class.

> *Imagine yourself at your kitchen table, in your pajamas. Imagine one person you'd allow to see you that way, and write in the voice you'd use to that friend.*
>
> Sandra Cisneros

Week One

Tell personal stories. It's tempting to tell the most amazing thing that ever happened to you—your high school band playing music for the President at the White House, maybe. It may be more helpful to tell everyday stories kids can relate to—the time you had to go to school with a horrible haircut, for instance. When we tell our own personal stories, we signal to students that their personal stories are valuable as well.

Invite students to tell their stories out loud. Here the "Think-Pair-Share" idea works very well. First, ask students to think of a story. Then pair off students and give them ten minutes to tell each other their stories. Finally, invite students to tell the story to the class. Students often can "talk story" pretty well. When they get a positive reaction from the class, they may be motivated to write the story.

Week Two

Read *Wilfrid Gordon McDonald Partridge* by Mem Fox. In this book the little boy puts objects from his life into a box, objects that stimulate an old woman's memory. Bring in a box or basket with objects from your own life: photographs, keepsakes, and things you have collected.

Share them with your students, and explain why they are important. Invite kids to bring their own "idea boxes" to school. The artifacts they bring in will also be great for sparking writing.

Create a writing ritual. A specific ritual—dimming the lights, turning on quiet music—signals to the students that this is our special time to write. Create one yourself, or solicit students' ideas.

Week Three

Invite students to write notes or "fan letters" to their peers who share. Let's say Antonio agrees to share his writing. Give students 3-by-5-inch index cards. Tell them to listen carefully to Antonio's story so they can jot him a note when he's finished. There should be three things on the note:

1. *Tell the writer what you liked about his or her piece. Don't just say: "That was good." Be specific!*

2. *Ask a question about something you wanted to know more about.*

3. *Sign your name.*

Notice that we leave off the note any suggestions for how the piece could be improved. When other students see Antonio receiving notes, they may be motivated to share, too.

Week Four

Have a writing celebration. Do this as early as possible in the Launch Cycle. You might invite students to stand around the room and "read into the circle." Let each student decide how much to read: a sentence, a paragraph, the whole piece. It's important to keep the tone upbeat and positive. Set the rules ahead of time—nothing but applause and accolades for whoever reads. You might suggest, "Hold the applause until the end."

Plan Your Way Through TQW

After the Launch Cycle you'll be ready to ask, What next? There are two basic ways to navigate TQW and choose the lessons you want to teach. Options 1 and 2 offer different levels of support.

Option 1: Choose Lessons by Cycle

The cycles provide a pre-arranged sequence to the lessons. Think of these cycles as building blocks that you arrange to create a yearlong curriculum of teaching the qualities. This option provides you with a large amount of our guidance; some teachers will prefer this level of support. Choose lessons based on the prearranged cycles to develop a road map for the school year.

Option 2: Choose Lessons by Teachers' and Students' Needs and Interests

Choose lessons based on your interest, your students' interests, and specific strengths and weaknesses you observe in your students' writing. Option 2 puts you totally in control of selecting and arranging the lessons.

In practice, most teachers will likely use these options in combination. The more you work with these materials, the more likely you are to find yourself reaching for the precise lesson that addresses the teachable moment before you. For now, we encourage you to read carefully through the next few pages as we take a closer look at each option.

I think of writing as a way of seeing. It's a way of bringing out the specialness of ordinary things.

– Laurence Yep

Option 1: Choose Lessons by Cycle

A poem demands a sense of order and design as much as a piece of nonfiction or a fictional narrative does. And all three benefit from fresh and clutter-free language. Few lessons are tied to specific genres, and as you familiarize yourself with the lessons, you will see that most can be used as students write in a variety of genres. Still, the lessons can easily be organized to teach students about the four qualities within the context of a specific genre study. Option 1 provides you with that organization. We offer a variety of prearranged genre studies, or cycles. You can use these cycles to navigate your way through the school year.

The Basic Road Map shows you how to select cycles to build a yearlong program:

The Basic Road Map

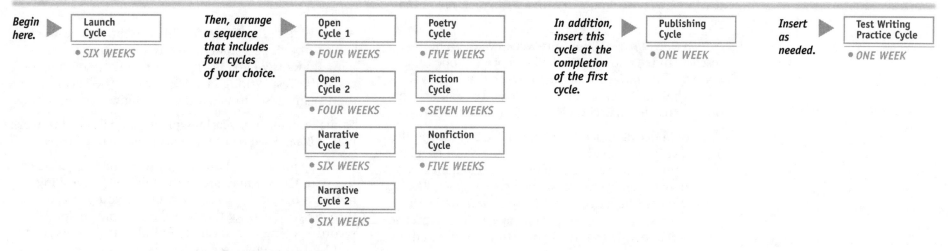

As you can see, you will need to choose from among the cycles that are offered—you simply cannot do all of them. Here is **one possible TQW Road Map** for your school year:

A Sample Road Map

Note that the Sample Road Map includes:

• *Two specified cycles.* Teachers may choose either poetry, nonfiction, fiction, or narrative. During these cycles, the teacher leads the entire class in a focused study of that genre.

• *Two Open Cycles.* These four-week cycles do not restrict students to one particular genre but open the doors for them to choose the form their writing will take. They can write in any and all genres, not just the one the teacher has chosen as a class focus.

You could decide to lead students through four specific genre cycles. However, to preserve the crucial element of student choice, we recommend you maintain a balance between specific and open genre cycles. The Instructional Challenge Chart (described in detail in Option 2) is a useful resource for suggesting the precise lessons that address some of your students' needs during the open cycles.

• *A Publishing Cycle immediately following the Open Cycle 1.* While students have taken some pieces of writing to final form during the Launch Cycle, the Publishing Cycle formally introduces students to the process of publishing. After this initial cycle, students will continue publishing independently in various ways throughout the year (roughly two or three times per quarter).

• *Test Writing Practice Cycle.* This very brief (one-week) walk-through gets students ready for a writing test. If your students will be taking a writing test, you might teach the Test Writing Practice Cycle in the fall, and then again closer to when the test is given in the spring.

To make your own yearlong plan, you will need to work with **a Blank Road Map** that looks like the one below.

You may prefer to fill out this form at the beginning of the year. Or you may prefer the flexibility of leaving part of it open so you can fill it out as you proceed through the year. All these road maps, plus helpful record-keeping forms, can be found in the Assessment and Record-keeping section on the CD and here in the Teacher's Guide. (See Appendix D).

A Blank Road Map

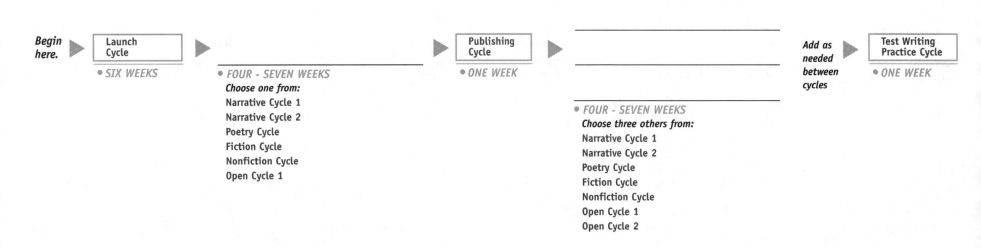

Begin here. → Launch Cycle → _____

• SIX WEEKS
• FOUR - SEVEN WEEKS
Choose one from:
Narrative Cycle 1
Narrative Cycle 2
Poetry Cycle
Fiction Cycle
Nonfiction Cycle
Open Cycle 1

→ Publishing Cycle → _____

• ONE WEEK

_____

• FOUR - SEVEN WEEKS
Choose three others from:
Narrative Cycle 1
Narrative Cycle 2
Poetry Cycle
Fiction Cycle
Nonfiction Cycle
Open Cycle 1
Open Cycle 2

Add as needed between cycles → Test Writing Practice Cycle

• ONE WEEK

If you intend to teach the Qualities of Writing through various genre cycles, consider these guidelines:

GUIDELINES FOR A GENRE STUDY

- Select beginning and ending dates and announce these dates to the class. If you have at least three writing workshops per week, most cycles will last between four and six weeks.

- Gather a wide variety of models (published texts) for the genre.

- Begin by reading these texts and discussing them with your students. Together with your students, build a list of the characteristics of the genre.

- Encourage students to generate ideas for topics about which they could write.

- Don't "front-load" the genre by teaching too much. Get students writing quickly, and teach information about the genre as they write.

- Teach focused lessons that address issues particular to this genre, in terms of both process and product.

- Be an example for your students. Model your own writing in this genre.

- As the ending date nears, invite students to select their favorite pieces. Prepare for a sharing/celebration.

- Make time to assess. Encourage students to select the piece they feel shows their best work in the genre. Ask them to select one other that shows them attempting a new technique, whether it was successful or not. Have students share their assessments with you and/or their peers. You may use the End-of-Cycle Assessment Form (see pages 63-69) to reflect on student growth.

Cycles Up Close and Personal

Narrative Cycles

Put two strangers together and before you know it they are swapping stories. We are natural storytellers. From the earliest years, children are steeped in narrative. They learn that telling the right story gives them a powerful way to shape their world.

The same holds true for writing. Story has been called the "mother of all genres." Indeed, elements of story show up in every genre you can imagine. If you decide to teach story early in the year (which we recommend), it makes sense to focus on personal narrative/memoir. There are several arguments for this:

Don Murray asserts that good writing begins with "honest, specific, accurate information." Personal narrative puts students in a realm where they can bring to the table those specific details that make the writing come alive.

Personal narrative creates a tension between what you remember (what is in your head) and what you have written on the page. This tension encourages students to revise. For this reason personal narrative is a good genre in which to help beginning writers learn the cycle of craft all writers go through.

Personal narrative continues to build community as students share stories that reveal their lives and allow them to learn about each other.

Because it provides such a natural way to begin, personal narrative has sometimes been taken for granted by teachers who simply want students to write while they organize the writing workshop. But this is a genre where we can stretch students.

Narrative 1

In Narrative Cycle 1, we introduce elements of story that will strengthen your students' writing, including character development, setting, leads and endings, details that develop an idea, pace dialogue, etc.

As you teach these lessons, think of these elements as tools. Students will choose when to pick them up and apply them to their writing. It is still the students' personal stories—not the lessons—that will generate the energy for this and every cycle in TQW.

- **Publishing Possibilities:** class anthology, authors' tea, visit to another class, schoolwide authors' day

Narrative 2

Most likely your students have worked through Narrative Cycle 1 earlier in the year. Or perhaps they were exposed to that cycle last year. Either way, you're ready to lead them into deeper waters in the Narrative Cycle 2.

This cycle, like the first narrative cycle, focuses on several story elements: beginnings, endings, focus, details. In addition, it touches on a range of punctuation—the dash, colon, and semicolon—allowing students to develop their sentence-writing skills.

- **Publishing Possibilities:** class anthology, authors' tea, visit to another class, schoolwide authors' day

Narrative Cycle 1

● WEEK ONE
- I-8 **Use Plot, Place, and Character in a Story**
- I-22 **Bring Your Characters to Life** *OR* I-25 **Develop Your Characters**
- I-23 **Describe What Your Characters Look Like**

● WEEK TWO
- I-24 **Develop the Inner Story**
- I-27 **Use Details to Bring the Setting Alive**
- D-3 **Organize Your Writing**

● WEEK THREE
- D-21 **Write a Lively Lead**
- D-22 **Write a Waterfall Lead**
- D-23 **Come Up with the Right Ending**

● WEEK FOUR
- I-15 **Use General Information and Specific Details**
- L-9 **Use Fresh Language**
- P-5 **Use Parentheses to Add Information**

● WEEK FIVE
- D-29 **Develop a Scene**
- L-19 **Write Believable Dialogue**
- P-14 **Break a Text into Paragraphs**

● WEEK SIX
- L-13 **Vary Sentence Beginnings**
- P-15 **Stop the Run-on Sentence**
- P-16 **Use Consistent Tense**

Narrative Cycle 2

● WEEK ONE
- I-8 **Use Plot, Place, and Character in a Story**
- D-13 **Use a Double Focus in a Narrative**
- D-31 **Use Details to Alter the Pace of Time**

● WEEK TWO
- D-4 **Use a Recurring Detail**
- D-33 **Use a Symmetrical Design**
- D-7 **Use the 2-3-1 Format for Organization**

● WEEK THREE
- **Choose** *ONE* **of the lessons on Leads (D-17, D-18, D-19, D-20, D-21, D-22)**
- **Choose** *ONE* **of the lessons on Endings (D-23, D-24, D-25, D-26)**
- L-17 **Tighten Dialogue**

● WEEK FOUR
- I-13 **Invent Specifics to Fill In Memory Gaps**
- I-16 **Use Inference to Let Readers Fill In the Gap**
- L-12 **Move from Simple to Complex Sentences**

● WEEK FIVE
- L-7 **Try Repetition in Narrative Writing**
- P-3 **Use Commas to Add an Aside** *OR* P-6 **Use the Dash to Spotlight Part of a Sentence**
- P-1 **Use a Colon to Introduce a List or Idea** *OR* P-2 **Use a Semicolon to Pull Together Related Sentences**

● WEEK SIX
- L-2 **Avoid Redundant Words**
- L-1 **Avoid Confusing Pronouns**
- P-9 **Edit for Passive Voice**

Poetry

Poetry is a
run on
sentence
that can go on
forever
It's smooth
sliding on your
tongue

by Allison Herschlein

The Poetry Cycle

Students like Allison are itching to write poetry. Other kids are less enthusiastic (or even hostile). Nevertheless, there are solid reasons to have your class concentrate on writing poetry for a few weeks:

- *Poems provide a context for talking about careful word choice. Every word matters in a poem. Writing poetry will help students write well in other genres. As Grace Paley said, "Poetry is the school I went to in order to learn to write prose."*

- *Poetry is short and punchy. Kids can finish a poem during a class period. If it doesn't work out, they know they'll have a fresh start the following day.*

- *It's easier to teach revision with a short text like a poem, since there are fewer words to work with.*

- *Even students who aren't enthusiastic about poetry are often surprised to find that it can be fun.*

This genre often gets taught as a series of poetic forms: haiku, limerick, sonnet, etc. That approach can result in a preoccupation with rules. The lessons you'll find here focus on free verse, with the main goal of helping students get a feel for poetry.

How to get started? Begin by reading some of your favorite nonrhyming poems. (See Bibliography, Appendix C). Gather ten or twenty poetry books of free verse and give students time to look through them, finding poems that speak to them. Devoting one or two class periods to exploring books like this will pay big dividends in the poetry students end up writing.

Poetry Cycle

• WEEK ONE	• WEEK TWO	• WEEK THREE	• WEEK FOUR	• WEEK FIVE
○ I-3 **Create a Poem with Imagery, Emotion, and Music**	○ D-14 **Use a Double Focus in a Poem**	○ L-8 **Use Alliteration**	○ D-26 **End with Your Strongest Line**	○ P-17 **Use Fragments When You Write a Poem**
○ I-2 **Create a Poem from a Story**	○ L-6 **Create Line Breaks in a Poem**	○ L-5 **Choose Words That Sound Like What They Mean**	○ D-8 **Use White Space in a Poem**	○ L-3 **Delete the Weak Parts**
○ I-20 **Use a Metaphor**	○ L-10 **Use Repetition in Poetry**	○ L-20 **Use a Thesaurus to Find Just the Right Word**	○ I-21 **Use Personification**	○ L-15 **Avoid Clichés**

Poems are fire for the cold, ropes let down to the lost, something as necessary as bread in the pockets of the hungry.

Mary Oliver

Continue to read aloud poems that you like, and get in the habit of reading them twice. Poetry is a dense kind of language that the ears can't always "digest" the first time around.

Do whatever you can to make students comfortable with poetry. Invite them to gather favorite poems they find in a special notebook. If it's feasible, make copies of selected poems and invite students to mark them up by circling or underlining favorite lines, surprising images, and reactions. You might divide them into groups of three or four and invite groups to do a choral reading of a poem.

The lessons that kick off each writing session in this cycle are designed to provide substance to your mini-lessons. Think of them as focused experimentations to help stretch young poets. At the end of this cycle, be sure to build in time for a celebration.

Some students may never have written poems before. They will feel exposed and vulnerable. Be gentle. You might begin the cycle by telling students, "You'll probably end up writing ten or twelve poems, maybe more, during these next few weeks. Some will be better than others. That's okay. I hope you'll experiment, borrow ideas from poems you read, and try different strategies that I throw out. We're going to have fun with this." As in everything, certain students will shine at writing poems. Your job is to find something wonderful in every student's work and point it out.

• **Publishing Possibilities:** poster, chap book, poetry jam, a class anthology, recitations, visiting poets, poem-in-a-pocket, published poem tucked in the cover of a book

The Fiction Cycle

When it comes to writing fiction, our students present us with a paradox. Since they love to read fiction, it's no wonder that they are eager to try their hands at this genre. But there is a major mismatch between what they typically read (novels) and what they write (very short stories). Books like *Harry Potter* don't provide very good models for how to write a story in a small number of pages.

For this reason, when you marinate your students in fiction, try to seek out pieces of short fiction that reflect the kind of fiction students write. (See Bibliography, Appendix C). Short stories by Gary Soto, Jacqueline Woodson, Cynthia Rylant, as well as selected picture books, will give kids an image of what they might shoot for.

This cycle assumes that students have already worked with the lessons that appear in the Launch and Narrative Cycles. Notice that we include only one lesson on character development and none on setting. It's not that character and setting aren't important in fiction writing. We trust students have learned about these elements in earlier cycles.

If you haven't worked with either of the narrative cycles, or if you think students need to revisit earlier ideas, include some of the lessons on character and setting from earlier cycles. In the fiction cycle we introduce and develop two new ideas: point of view and story shape.

Writing fiction is a bit like surfing a wave—it's a lot harder than it looks. This doesn't mean you shouldn't give students a chance to write fiction. But you need to be realistic and generous when their writing doesn't live up to your expectations. Make sure you point out strengths in their writing.

- **Publishing Possibilities:** story shelf in classroom library or the main office, books donated to local doctors' offices waiting rooms, a class anthology of short stories (themed or not), visiting authors get-together, hosting storytime lunch or snack.

Fiction Cycle

WEEK ONE	WEEK TWO	WEEK THREE	WEEK FOUR	WEEK FIVE	WEEK SIX	WEEK SEVEN
I-8 Use Plot, Place, and Character in a Story	I-29 Work with an Internal Conflict	I-30 Write in the First Person	D-28 Create Suspense in Fiction	D-34 Use a Triangular Structure	D-17 Cut to Your Lead	L-4 Remove Those Annoying Little Qualifiers
I-11 Embellish an Idea	I-18 Value Your Experience	I-31 Write in the Second Person	D-27 Control How Time Moves	D-32 Use a Snapshot Structure	D-19 Lead with the Big Picture	L-11 Combine Short Sentences
I-28 Work with an External Conflict	I-26 Make Your Story Believable	I-32 Write in the Third Person		D-35 Write a Circular Story or Poem	Choose ONE of the lessons on endings (D-23, D-24, D-25, D-26)	L-14 Vary the Length of Sentences

The Nonfiction Cycle

"When a tornado hits a house," one fifth grader explained to his class, "the roof might get torn off, but bathtubs and toilets almost always stay put."

"How come?" one girl asked. But the whole class wanted to know.

"Because they're bolted down to pipes that go way down into the ground," the boy explained.

Kids are fascinated by the workings of the world: venomous spiders, coelacanth fossils, typhoons and tsunamis, underground lava rivers, giant squid, mummified cats in ancient Egypt….Alas, this passion for the world doesn't always find an outlet in the nonfiction writing they do in school. Of all the genres they encounter, nonfiction is the one that most typically gets "done to" students. We tell them what to write about, we give them a detailed outline, we impose a system for note-taking and research, and then we grade the result. This kind of approach puts students in a passive role. No wonder we often encounter "dump truck writing" in this genre.

It's important to make students active participants as they explore and explain the world around them. We should give them as much choice as possible, in terms of both *what* to write about and *how* to present the material. This makes it easier for them to bring their natural voice into this genre.

This cycle consists of fifteen lessons to help students write nonfiction. The lessons assume that students are ready to write about their topics. Any needed research should already have been done before you begin with the lessons in Week 1.

Nonfiction writing challenges students first to learn about their topic and then to communicate what they have learned to readers. Several lessons provide guidance for students during the research process. These include:

- *Anticipate What the Audience Expects*
- *Use Subtitles to Organize Your Writing*
- *Use Vocabulary Specific to a Subject*
- *Make a Comparison*

Nonfiction Cycle

WEEK ONE
- L-18 **Use a Natural Voice**
- D-10 **Find the Right Distance by Pulling in Close**
- D-11 **Find the Right Distance by Pulling Back**

WEEK TWO
- D-1 **Anticipate What the Audience Expects**
- D-9 **Capture the Power of One**
- I-14 **Use Authentic Details**

WEEK THREE
- D-6 **Use Subtitles to Organize Your Writing**
- D-20 **Open with a Scene**
- D-18 **Lead with a Question**

WEEK FOUR
- L-24 **Use Vocabulary Specific to a Subject**
- D-5 **Use a Transition Between Ideas**
- I-19 **Make a Comparison**

WEEK FIVE
- P-4 **Use Commas to List Ideas**
- P-7 **Use the Ellipsis**
- L-16 **Avoid Passive Verbs**

Students cannot write in a vacuum. Therefore, it makes sense to begin this cycle by devoting at least one period to exploring the many techniques professional writers use in nonfiction writing. Pass around a few dozen exemplary nonfiction texts (see Bibliography, Appendix C), asking students to read through them. During this time you'll notice students paying attention to photographs and captions, drawings, close-up illustrations, charts, graphs, and lists. Remind students that they can include all of these in their finished products.

Nonfiction is an important kind of writing. The students write varieties of nonfiction right through their senior year in college and beyond. It's also probably the genre most used in the workplace. These lessons provide a solid introduction to the genre. But let's not be so ambitious with teaching strategies/techniques that we forget that the students' wonder, passions, and obsessions are the most crucial ingredients in this genre.

- **Publishing Possibilities:** information brochure, report, bulletin board display, teaching poster, explanatory text posted next to projects, museum exhibit, event, or object description, multigenre research project, oral report or debate, feature article

Keep listening. Keep your radar out. Take everything, because it is matter for your work. No detail is too small.

Mary Tallmountain

The Publishing Cycle

Kids are motivated to go to soccer practice because they know they're going to play actual soccer games. Kids practice their lines for a play because they realize that there will be a real production before a real audience. Students write partly out of the sheer joy of expressing themselves but also because they want to communicate their thoughts to real readers. Publishing means no more than that—helping students find a wider audience for what they have written.

There are many reasons why students must go public with their written work. Publishing gives students an authentic context for using skills—editing, spelling, grammar—and for getting it right. It teaches them the concept of permanence—once their words have been published, they must live with the decisions they made while drafting. Some students need the first go-round with publishing before they truly understand the importance of revising for a distant reader.

This cycle assumes students are publishing for the first time during the school year (though they may have published during the previous year). If your students have been working with TQW for several years, you may choose not to begin with the introductory lesson.

You may decide to lead your class as a group through the publishing process the first time. Or you may prefer to begin by helping individual students or small groups of students. After this first cycle, students should publish individually when they are ready.

There are five lessons in this cycle. If you limit the publishing cycle to one week, you'll probably choose three of these lessons. Later on you can present to your class the other lessons you didn't use the first time around.

Publishing Cycle

- P-19 **Choose What Gets Published**
- P-12 **Personalize the Editing Checklist**
- P-18 **Choose an Appropriate Form**
- P-20 **Create Illustrations for the Text**
- P-21 **Reflect on Your Writing**

When you think of final form, don't be limited to the walls of the classroom. Find places in the larger school and community for student writing to be read. Help students find the natural audience for what they have written. Ask them, "Can you think of a relative or someone who would like to read this?" Encourage students to send the finished piece to that person.

Some schools have publishing centers that turn out glossy books. That's a wonderful resource, but make sure students don't see this as the only way to publish. You may want to set up a publishing center in your own classroom. If you do, you will need certain materials that suggest the range of ways to present writing:

Materials for Publishing

- *Markers and colored pencils*
- *Variety of paper*
- *Guidelines for printing straight rows*
- *Various media for illustrations: watercolors, gauche, paper scraps*
- *Calligraphy pens*
- *Book-making supplies: dental floss, cardboard, wallpaper*
- *Premade blank books*

Each cycle brings its own publishing challenges and possibilities (see Appendix B). Don't be bound by these lists; use your creativity to devise other ways.

"But my students aren't ready to publish!" teachers often say. Don't fall into the trap of setting your sights too high. The publishing process gives students important knowledge that will impact their writing throughout the year. For this reason, we suggest you publish early and often.

- **Publishing** doesn't require you to stay up till midnight binding students' books with dental floss. It can be as simple as having students do a final draft, walking down the hall, and reading it to another class. It's important that they see their words rippling out into the world.

*I seek words,
I chase after them.
When I write I'm
trying to put the most
beautiful words in
the world down
on paper.*

Cynthia Rylant

Open Cycles 1 and 2

Writers are people who make decisions. This tenet holds true for writers of every age. John Poeton reminds us that "choice leads to voice in writing." But curricular realities sometimes limit how much choice we allow students. We recognize that many teachers who bring TQW into their classrooms will move students through various "writing seasons" that focus on particular genres. Indeed, we have suggested lesson sequences for these cycles.

There are good arguments for moving your class through various genre studies (being able to draw on common literature, for instance), but there are certain drawbacks to this approach. Ideally, and in the most organic sense, content should precede form. In other words, the idea itself should suggest whether a piece would best be written as a poem, feature article, etc. This does not happen when students already know what genre in which they'll be writing.

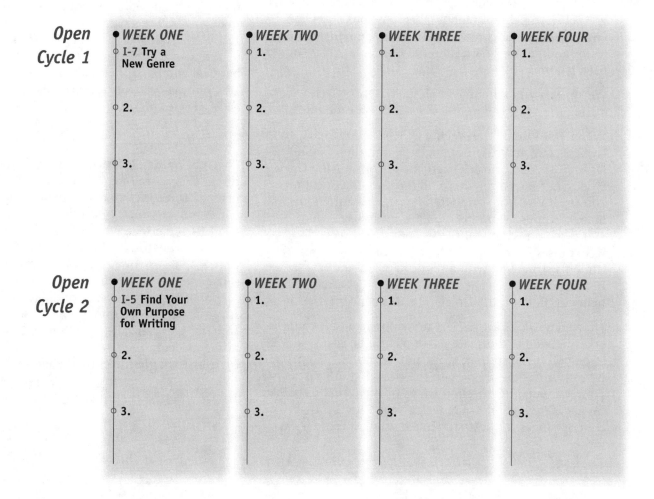

Open Cycle 1

● WEEK ONE	● WEEK TWO	● WEEK THREE	● WEEK FOUR
I-7 **Try a New Genre**	1.	1.	1.
2.	2.	2.	2.
3.	3.	3.	3.

Open Cycle 2

● WEEK ONE	● WEEK TWO	● WEEK THREE	● WEEK FOUR
I-5 **Find Your Own Purpose for Writing**	1.	1.	1.
2.	2.	2.	2.
3.	3.	3.	3.

In the Open Cycles students can exercise choice to the fullest. Here we don't impose genre restrictions. Instead, we open the door and let students make the crucial decisions:

- *What am I going to write about?*
- *Who will I want to read this?*
- *What form (or genre) should this writing take?*

If you want to affect young writers, you have to let their writing affect you. The Open Cycles give you a chance to let your students' writing do that. Now is the time to be a generous reader, to appreciate their wit and humor, to delight in their work. Chances are good that students will relish this time to follow their passions and play with language. Encourage them to experiment with forms and perhaps try a kind of writing they have never tried before.

We suggest you schedule at least two Open Cycles during the year. Different lessons kick off each one.

When you look at the weekly cycle plan for the Open Cycles, your first reaction might be: but there are no lessons! That's not true. There are lessons for the Open Cycles, but it's up to you to fill them in. We encourage you to choose from any other lessons from the four main qualities. Naturally, you'll want to base what you teach on what you see — both strengths and weaknesses — in your students' writing. If you see students struggling with a particular skill, the Instructional Challenge Chart (pages 41-43) may help you find a lesson to address this concern.

The Open Cycles are a great time to read aloud your favorite poems, short stories, or picture books, or to take strong pieces of student work and, with the students' permission, share them with the class. In both cases, ask your students the question we want them to internalize, "What is this writer doing well?" These texts provide concrete ideas for how students can enhance their own writing.

The Test Writing Practice Cycle

Test writing is stressful for both students and teachers. Everybody reacts to it in different ways. Some teachers get so worried about the test, they feed students a steady diet of prompts from the first week of school. Others ignore it for as long as possible.

It's probably best to steer a middle course. Remember: there is no quick fix for building strong writers in your class. Students who write on a regular basis (at least three times a week) and who receive regular instruction in writing (including regular writing conferences) need not be intimidated by a writing test. For this reason, we urge you: *don't sacrifice your curriculum on the altar of the state writing test.* On the other hand, it makes sense to take reasonable measures to ensure that your students perform competently on such a test. That's where the Test Writing Practice Cycle comes in. *This cycle is not designed to teach students new ideas for writing. Rather, it is designed to help your students practice so they can write well under test conditions.*

The Test Writing Practice Cycle should last about one week. Consider doing one cycle in the fall and another just before the actual test. Each time you will begin with a lesson using *Read, Underline the prompt, Plan, Revise* (R-U-P-R), an idea we got from Pat Thompson. R-U-P-R is a great way to get kids comfortable with the prompt. Rather than use one of our prompts, it makes most sense for you to use the prompts typically used by your school or state. For the second day of the cycle, we suggest you choose one of four lessons that deal with content. The third day's lesson focuses on mechanics. Students begin their writing on the second day of this cycle and should finish by the end of the week.

The Test Writing Practice Cycle

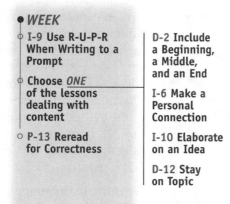

WEEK

I-9 Use R-U-P-R When Writing to a Prompt

Choose ONE of the lessons dealing with content

P-13 Reread for Correctness

D-2 Include a Beginning, a Middle, and an End

I-6 Make a Personal Connection

I-10 Elaborate on an Idea

D-12 Stay on Topic

The first time you walk students through this cycle, try to be very relaxed about it. If you return to this cycle just before the test, you'll want to give them at least one opportunity to write to a prompt under actual test conditions.

Whatever calm you can bring to this cycle will reap benefits in your students' attitudes and performance. Remind students that although writing to a test prompt does differ from writing in a workshop, it still boils down to getting your ideas down on paper in the best way possible so readers can understand what you're trying to say. Everything you have taught them about what makes good writing—strong leads, focus, transitions, supporting details, etc.—also holds true for the writing test.

Option 2: Choose Lessons by Teacher and Student Need and Interest

Let's remember our earlier assumption: students learn to write by writing. The materials in TQW assume that your students have regular time to write. So you might simply read through the lesson titles over the course of the year and choose the ones that interest you and your students. If you are new to talking about the Qualities of Writing, the lessons will help you initiate the kind of conversation that helps students think like writers. With this approach it's likely that you will also search for lessons that address the specific needs your students' writing presents. To guide you in this practice, we provide you with three resources:

- *Looking-at-Student-Writing CD-ROM*
- *The Instructional Challenge Chart*
- *Assessment and Record-keeping Forms*

Looking-at-Student-Writing CD-ROM

This tutorial gives you a chance to listen in as we discuss 24 pieces of writing from students in grades three through six. We have chosen student writing samples that, we believe, reflect the kind of writing you will encounter in your own settings. The CD invites you to pull a chair up to the table while we talk about what we see as the qualities (strengths and weaknesses) in student drafts. Although our discussions vary somewhat, you'll note that in general we point out both strengths in the writing and one or two areas where the student needs work.

As teachers we read student work through an appreciative and critical lens because we want to know how to stretch the writer to new levels of quality. We believe you will find it helpful to look over our shoulders and listen in while we discuss writing by students in a range of genres, and with a range of abilities. Our ultimate goal is to help you develop wiser ways of looking at your own students' writing.

The Instructional Challenge Chart

The Instructional Challenge Chart provides examples of some of the most common problems you will encounter in your students' writing and references the TQW lessons that address them. As you become familiar with the full range of TQW lessons and your own students' writing difficulties, you will become adept at matching specific lessons to specific student needs. Here's how the chart works.

Let's say you notice that your students' writing tends to be rather skimpy. They write quickly without adding a lot of detail. When you look at the chart, you'll find a problem listed as "too little information." Yep, you think, that describes what I see. But we can look at "too little information" even more specifically. In the excerpt on page 44, there are five possible descriptions that help refine the problem you're seeing. If one fits your writers, read across to the next column and you'll find a list of TQW lessons that will help address that issue. The third column lists the title of one or more student writing samples found on the *Looking-at-Student-Writing* CD. If you like, visit that portion of the CD to hear us talk about this weakness in the context of a specific piece of writing.

Option 2 relies on a continuous feedback loop. The students write, you observe and read their writing, and then you select and teach the appropriate TQW lessons based on your observations. Students continue to write and you continue to listen and observe. In addition to serving as a troubleshooter, the Instructional Challenge Chart demonstrates, using 24 writing samples offered on the CD, how we would move from reading and assessing student writing to selecting and teaching a TQW lesson.

Learning to document, analyze, and use assessment data is the hallmark of a professional teacher. Through the *Looking-at-Student-Writing* CD and Instructional Challenge Chart we show you the ways in which we analyze, document, and use assessment data to inform your instruction. This is the teaching-assessment loop in action, and it's a loop you may want to learn to use in your own classroom. These resources will help you to that end.

The beautiful part of writing is that you don't have to get it right the first time, unlike, say, a brain surgeon. You can always do it better, find the exact word, the apt phrase, the leaping simile.

Robert Cormier

Instructional Challenge Chart

IDEAS STUDENT WRITING CHALLENGES	RELEVANT TQW LESSONS AND HELPFUL CLASSROOM SUGGESTIONS	STUDENT WRITING ON THE CD-ROM
too little information *provides a skeletal telling of an event*	**I-11** *Embellish an Idea,* **I-10** *Elaborate on an Idea,* **I-25** *Develop Your Characters,* **D-29** *Develop a Scene,* **D-31** *Use Details to Alter the Pace of Time,* **D-27** *Control* *How Time Moves*	The Bonfire; My Dog River's Life
lacks details needed to create a sense of place or point of view	**I-14** *Use Authentic Details,* **I-12** *Free Write for Specifics,* **D-30** *Find Your Focus*	My Dog River's Life; Creepy Place
introduces an idea but fails to develop it	**I-17** *Use Supporting Details*	Being a Twin
has a richer understanding in his or her head than appears on the page	**D-10** *Find the Right Distance by Pulling in Close,* **D-11** *Find the Right Distance by Pulling Back,* **D-1** *Anticipate What the Audience Expects*	Army Men
leaves out information the reader needs to understand	*This skill relies on the writer's ability to read as an outside reader. Provide an audience (a peer, the class, yourself) and coach the student to use the reader's questions to clarify the writing.*	A Union Troop's Journal; The Sweet Smell of Rotten Bananas, Toilet Water, and Success
includes info the reader doesn't need	**I-16** *Use Inference to Let Readers Fill In the Gap*	The Viper
implausible fiction	**I-26** *Make Your Story Believable,* **I-18** *Value Your Experience*	Longing for Indiana
inaccurate information	**I-26** *Make Your Story Believable,* **I-14** *Use Authentic Details*	A Union Troop's Journal
underdeveloped characterization *introduces characters without fully developing them*	**I-25** *Develop Your Characters,* **I-23** *Describe What Your Character Look Like,* **I-22** *Bring Your Characters to Life*	Army Men
needs to develop the narrator as a character	**I-24** *Develop the Inner Story,* **I-25** *Develop Your Characters* **I-6** *Make a Personal Connection,* **D-10** *Find the Right Distance by Pulling in Close*	The Bonfire; A Union Troop's Journal

DESIGN STUDENT WRITING CHALLENGES	RELEVANT TQW LESSONS AND HELPFUL CLASSROOM SUGGESTIONS	STUDENT WRITING ON THE CD-ROM
lacks focus *title misleads the reader*	*D-15 Use a Thematic Focus, D-16 Use a Time Focus*	The Shine
deals with the topic in a general way	*D-9 Capture the Power of One, D-15 Use a Thematic Focus, D-16 Use a Time Focus, D-10 Find the Right Distance by Pulling in Close, D-14 Use a Double Focus in a Narrative*	My Dog River's Life; The Red Kangaroo
ineffective ending *runs out of steam*	*D-26 End with Your Strongest Line*	Egg Disaster
writes an ending that doesn't live up to the rest of the writing	*Any lesson in D/Endings; Sometimes all the student needs is a break from the piece. Encourage the writer to put aside the work and return later with a fresh set of eyes.*	Attack of the Nachos; I Like to Use My Imagination
ends on a general note when a specific note would be stronger	*I-15 Use General Information and Specific Details*	Egg Disaster
lacks organization *has no clear beginning and/or ending*	*D-3 Organize Your Writing* *Any of the lessons in D/Beginnings or D/Endings*	Being a Twin
writes with little sense of organization	*D-3 Organize Your Writing, D-2 Include a Beginning, a Middle, and an End; D-6 Use Subtitles to Organize Your Writing; If student is writing fiction, lessons in Design/Shape may be helpful*	The Red Kangaroo
does not include "signposts" the reader might expect	*A "signpost" will be very specific to the form of writing, as in the case on the CD where the student writes a diary without dating the entries. When this occurs you can help by having the student look at authentic models of the form.*	A Union Troop's Journal

LANGUAGE STUDENT WRITING CHALLENGES	RELEVANT TQW LESSONS AND HELPFUL CLASSROOM SUGGESTIONS	STUDENT WRITING ON THE CD-ROM
• **limited word choice** ○ *chooses vague words*	*L-22 Use Precise Nouns, L-21 Use Choice Adjectives, L-24 Use Vocabulary Specific to a Subject*	The Shine
○ *writes with ordinary images or language*	*I-19 Make a Comparison, L-9 Use Fresh Language, I-15 Use General Information and Specific Details*	I Like to Use My Imagination
○ *uses limited vocabulary*	*L-20 Use a Thesaurus to Find Just the Right Word, L-23 Use Verbs That Describe Action, L-24 Use Vocabulary Specific to a Subject*	The Red Kangaroo
• **inconsistent text (some lines or images much stronger than others)**	*D-30 Find Your Focus, I-13 Invent Specifics to Fill In Memory Gaps*	Being a Twin
• **flat voice**	*L-9 Use Fresh Language, L-8 Use Alliteration, L-7 Try Repetition in Narrative Writing, L-18 Use a Natural Voice, I-6 Make a Personal Connection*	Five Things Cheetahs Do
• **repeats self or carries on too long**	*L-3 Delete the Weak Parts, L-2 Avoid Redundant Words*	It Was a Horrible Day; Ice Cream

PRESENTATION STUDENT WRITING CHALLENGES	RELEVANT TQW LESSONS AND HELPFUL CLASSROOM SUGGESTIONS	STUDENT WRITING ON THE CD-ROM
• **sentence level problems** ○ *writes complicated sentences that aren't properly punctuated*	*P-6 Use the Dash to Spotlight Part of a Sentence, P-2 Use a Semicolon to Pull Together Related Sentences. P-5 Use Parentheses to Add Information, L-11 Combine Short Sentences, L-12 Move from Simple to Complex Sentences*	It Was a Horrible Day; Ice Cream
○ *uses short, staccato sentences (or lacks sentence variety)*	*L-13 Vary Sentence Beginnings, L-14 Vary the Length of Sentences*	The Bonfire; The Red Kangaroo
○ *uses run-on sentences*	*P-15 Stop the Run-on Sentence*	Ice Cream
• **conventions** ○ *doesn't write in paragraphs*	*P-14 Break a Text into Paragraphs*	It Was a Horrible Day; My Dog River's Life
○ *doesn't use correctly punctuated dialogue*	*P-14 Break a Text into Paragraphs*	Attack of the Nachos

III The Continuous Assessment – Teaching Loop

Assessment and Record-keeping

Assessment, while key to effective instruction, can be a risk when valuable time for learning gets usurped by an overzealous attention to assessing growth. Because we believe students learn in the acts of reading, writing, and talking, the best assessment of their growth happens closest to these actions. Teachers who listen closely as students talk about their writing gain an understanding of their students' skills: assessment happens moment to moment. In addition to daily on-going observations, it helps to step back and take a slower look at a collection of a student's work over time.

Our goal in TQW is to incorporate assessment without letting the process sink the program of instruction. Still the challenge exists: How do I keep track of all I observe? That's where record keeping comes in.

The week before our son Robert left for camp, we started packing. Everything he needed would fit into our large green duffel bag. But where was the darn thing? We searched everywhere: the attic and basement storage rooms, the mud room closet downstairs, and Robert's bedroom closet upstairs (he had used it last). After four days of searching I (JoAnn) finally found it, folded and hidden under a pile of sweaters on the top shelf of the living room closet. During my search I had stopped to think, "where would I put a duffel bag if I were putting it away today?" That thought had led me to the living room closet. But it wasn't until my third visit that I dug deep enough to find it. Through it all, I lamented the inefficiency of our home organization system.

As a writing teacher you have a similar need to organize and retrieve information about your students and your teaching. Instead of a duffel bag, you might store the remnants of conversations with students or notes on a series of lessons you taught in October. When readily available, these records save precious time and put at your fingertips the information you need to make good instructional decisions.

You'll want to make your record-keeping simple. You can create a comprehensive system to record just about anything under the sun. But if the system is too complicated, you won't keep up with it. If you find a way to take quick and easy notes as you work, the system will practically run itself. Most of the forms included here can be carried on a clipboard as you work with students. Once you complete a sheet, file it in a three-ring binder. Before long you'll have what you need to take a longer, slower look at the year and your student's process.

Record-keeping systems vary from teacher to teacher. Only you know exactly what information you need, when you need it, and where you're most likely to reach for it. With that in mind we've offered you a variety of forms to choose from. We hope some will fit your purpose as written. If not, a little tweak should make the difference. We offer one important caution: *Do not plan to use more than a small handful of these.* A good system should be like invisible netting that keeps everything in place without calling attention to itself.

A Quick Tour of Tools for Assessing Student Writing

Tools That Link Assessment to Instruction

Instructional Challenge Chart (page 41)

Purpose: *Use to plan instruction based on specific needs present in student writing.*

When to use: *During Open Cycles and other times as needed.*

How to use: *Review student writing and refer to chart. Look for student indicators in the first column that match the needs of your students. Select from the referenced lessons to design a plan that meets the needs of your class.*

Teacher Assessment Form (page 62)

Purpose: *Use to reflect on a student's strengths and weaknesses across the four Qualities of Writing (Ideas, Design, Language, Presentation) and to plan instruction accordingly.*

When to use: *Quarterly throughout the school year or as needed.*

How to use: *Read through a collection of the student's work using the process we demonstrate on the Looking-at-Student-Writing CD-ROM. Identify strategies to use with individual students and/or look for common issues to address with the entire class.*

End of Cycle Assessment Form (page 63) *(a specific form for each cycle including a blank form to be completed by teacher for use with the Open Cycle)*

Purpose: *Use to assess student progress in terms of specific qualities presented in the genre cycle.*

When to use: *End of each genre cycle.*

How to use: *Read a collection of each student's work generated during the genre cycle. Make specific notes that demonstrate the student's success within each quality. Note any common concerns that can be addressed through future whole-class lessons.*

Tools That Track Instruction

Daily Record-keeping Form (page 70)

Purpose: *Use to record notes on your teaching.*

When to use: *Daily.*

How to use: *Use a new sheet for each writing lesson you teach. Record the lesson and text materials you plan to use. Keep brief notes on your daily student conferences. Jot notes for future lessons as you reflect on the day's lesson. Keep a week's worth of these on your clipboard and file them away at the end of each week in a three-ring binder. By June you'll have a detailed and revealing record of the year. While it can't serve as a precise road map for next year, it will give you a solid reference point as you work with a new group of writers.*

Week-at-a-Glance Form (page 71)

Purpose: *Same purpose as Daily Record-keeping Form but holds an entire week's record on a single page.*

Cycle-at-a-Glance Form (page 72) *(grid format or box format)*

Purpose: *Use to jot brief notes on each day's lessons (e.g., a plan to extend the lesson, names of student you will confer with next).*

When to use: *Daily during a given genre cycle.*

How to use: *Keep the form handy as you work each day. At the end of each session, jot notes to help guide the next day's work (students you wish to confer with, ideas for extending the lesson). Or try this: jot the names of students who attempt to use each strategy listed.*

Conference Record Sheet (page 84) *(by date and lesson for each genre cycle)*

Conference Record Sheet (page 94) *(by date)*

Purpose: *Use to keep tally of individual student conferences.*

When to use: *Daily as you work with students.*

How to use: *Carry on a clipboard and indicate when you confer with a student. This easy-to-check lists tracks who you've worked with.*

*If you prefer to write longer notes about student conferences, consider using index cards, a conference journal, or jot them on charts (See **Conference Chart, page 95**).*

Student Forms That Accompany Lessons

Uses of the Comma
(page 96)

*Accompanies **Use a Comma to Add an Aside** or **Use Commas to List Ideas**. Students record the various uses of the comma as they are taught or when they discover them in the context of their reading. The sheet stays in the student's writing folder for handy reference during editing.*

Writing Reflection
(page 99)

*Accompanies **Reflect on Your Writing**. Students use this form to reflect on their published work.*

Personal Word List
(page 97)

*Accompanies **Be Aware of Words You Commonly Misspell**. This editing resource helps students monitor their own spelling needs.*

Editing Checklist
(page 98)

*Accompanies **Edit with a Checklist**. A simple checklist introduces students to editing.*

IV In Your Classroom: The Resources You Need

Teaching writing isn't like teaching science or math. You don't have to organize and store boxes of manipulatives or equipment for science experiments. If you have access to a good library and a steady stream of student writing, you've got the most important resources you'll need.

Access to Books: Developing Your Classroom Library

You simply cannot teach writing without books. Books show students possibilities for their own writing and give them something to shoot for. A variety of rich texts will nourish students with "stretch language" that will keep them growing as writers.

You probably have access to the school (or local) library. But this is not a substitute for building your classroom library. A well-stocked library will give you texts you can quickly lay your hands upon when you want to teach one element of writing. We recognize that budgets everywhere are tight when it comes to books. You don't need hundreds and hundreds of texts; rather, see if you can't build a smaller collection of books that can directly impact the writers with whom you work.

Why Picture Books?

Many of the lessons use picture books as exemplar texts. This may seem surprising given the fact that most third to sixth grade students have already moved into reading chapter books. But picture books provide a powerful tool for teaching writing. Picture Story Books contain all the literary elements—protagonist, setting, tension, problem/resolution—that are found in novels. But unlike full-length novels, these books offer a model of how to develop these elements in a text similar in length to what most students write. And that's just the beginning. The picture book format holds the entire range of genres we hope students will try. Our experience has shown that picture books have a lovely transparency: they rely on a limited amount of text, which allows students to quickly grasp the writing strategy you want to teach.

How to Get the Books We Recommend

Most teachers have had to come up with many ingenious ways of getting books. Begin with your school library. Also, local libraries sometimes have book sales where they sell books at a fraction of their cost. You may want to team up with another teacher, pool your resources, and buy books that can be shared between the two writing classrooms. Tap other resources. Make a master list of books you'd like for your classroom and make it available for those opportunities when parents or students are looking to acknowledge you or the class.

What to Do If You Can't Get the Recommended Books

In most cases, when a lesson calls for a piece of literature, we've tried to draw on books that teachers will readily find in any elementary school library.

If you can't find the book we recommend, however, select an appropriate title of your own choosing or try the alternative titles we suggest. While some lessons are written around a particular recommended text, you'll find you can use our language as a guide as you substitute your text for ours.

Teacher Tools

Beyond the exemplar texts and children's literature, there are few materials you need. As you read the lessons you'll notice occasional references to necessary student or teacher materials. We list general things here so you see up front what's required. But none of the things on the list are essential.

Chart paper and markers

While you can always use a black board or white board in lieu of chart paper, we prefer recording demonstrations on paper that can be filed and returned to as needed.

Overhead projector

Typically, on the back of the lessons cards you'll find either 1) an exemplar text around which to base your lesson or 2) specific teaching instructions to which you may want to refer as you talk with your students about writing. If you have access to an overhead projector, you may choose to make transparencies of the back of the cards and use them while you teach.

Kitchen timer

Some lessons direct you to lead the class in a short focused writing warm-up. There's something about the certainty of the timer going off that makes it easier to try something for a limited time. It's a gadget that students seem to respond to.

Writing folders

Students need a way to organize and store their writing. This allows them to put a piece of writing aside (because they tire of it or can't make it work) and return to it later. Writing folders also provide you, students, and their parents with a yearlong history of their work. You may ask students to reflect on this history at the end of each marking period to assess their growth and to set goals for the next quarter. These folders are useful in helping parents see the richness of your writing curriculum while showcasing their child's developing writing skills.

The Writer's Lifeblood

Much of TQW operates on the microlevel. While we believe that it's important to teach students strategies to make them better writers, we shouldn't try to reduce writing to a few dozen techniques. It's helpful to step back every so often to look at the big picture. The Writer's Lifeblood contains powerful quotes about writing by professional writers. Here you'll find big ideas to inspire and sustain the spirit of the young writers with whom you work. There are twenty-eight of them, selected in the belief that they will speak to the young writer's heart. If nurturing strong writers remains our long-range goal, these quotes may be as important as the individual lessons.

Download them from the CD or look for them at the back of this Teacher's Guide (Appendix A). You can enlarge the quotes on a photocopy machine and create posters. Post them on your walls and make time for students to respond to these writers' words. These quotes can lead to interesting conversation, and help students see themselves in the larger world of writers.

As you consider the challenges your English Language Learners face daily, you may want to acquaint yourself with the strategies and techniques that help English Language Learners access lessons in English. Chances are you're already implementing many of these strategies in your classroom. What's more, as you read through the TQW lessons, you'll see how you might easily incorporate these techniques into your teaching.

ENGLISH LANGUAGE LEARNER GUIDELINES

- **Reduce anxiety.**
Stephen Krashen and Tracy Terrell (1983) remind us that students acquire a second language when the linguistic input is comprehensible and the affective filter that controls our emotions is not interfering. In other words, as our stress levels increase, our affective filter effectively blocks out all new, incoming information—including our target language. Fear, like static, is a great inhibiter. Learning flows only when all channels are open, receptive, and static-free.

- **Create a predictable classroom routine.**
Certainly, one great stress reducer is a predictable classroom structure and schedule—the great advantage of a smooth-running writing workshop (see Fletcher & Portalupi 2001). English Language Learners may not understand everything that's going on around them. Writing workshop's predictable routine and simple structure enable students to relax. They don't have to worry about what might happen next so they can concentrate on your instruction.

- **Arrange for small collaborative work groups and language buddies.**
English Language Learners need lots of interaction and a small-group setting typically feels safer and more supportive than whole-class instruction. You can further enhance small-group work by pairing language buddies. Ideally, you pair two students with the same primary language so the more competent English speaker can translate and interpret for his or her partner. But even a sensitive English speaker can guide a student who's learning English simply by paying close attention to his or her buddy's needs and intervening as needed.

- **Call on your community.**
Don't forget community help! Use to the fullest extent possible cross-age tutors, bilingual parents, community volunteers, and college students—anyone from or beyond the school who's willing to translate and assist. You alone can never provide all the one-on-one support your English Language Learners need. And your multilingual helpers can do what you may not be able to do: field questions, explain challenging concepts, or participate in an extended conversation.

- **Use visual prompts and show-and-tell modeling.**
Whenever possible, use prompts—drawings, charts, overheads, maps, photographs, and other authentic artifacts. Visual aids help build concrete context and provide English Language Learners multiple entry points into the meaning of English instruction. And showing and telling—acting out your message—often goes hand in hand with visual prompts. Don't just tell a story—use hand gestures and dramatic flourishes to help your English Language Learners comprehend your message (Cary, 2000).

- **Honor native languages.**
Surround your students with their native language—for every quote you post in English, consider posting the identical quote or a similar inspirational saying in your English Language Learners' primary languages (ask parents and community volunteers to translate). As you are able to do so, bring in written materials such as dictionaries, picture books, newspapers, and other resources in your English Language Learners' native languages. If your students are recent arrivals to the States, you'll want to encourage them to write in their native tongue until their oral English improves. Rely on bilingual students, parents, or community volunteers to translate for you. Otherwise, encourage your English Language Learners to write in English while, at the same time, inviting them to write, as they are moved to do so, in their own language. By honoring the native languages represented in your classroom, you drive home the message that knowing two languages or more is better than one.

A Word About Your Daily Writing Schedule

In a perfect world students come to school every day knowing they will have sustained time to write on the topics and projects that matter to them. Most of us live in a less-than-perfect world and so we juggle multiple needs while trying to hold on to a few key principles.

Reread the first core belief at the heart of TQW and you'll find our advice that you offer students sustained time (25–35 minutes of writing stretches three to five times a week) where they are deeply engaged in the act of writing.

Following this advice, you may dedicate a 50-to 60-minute block for writing three days a week. You'll begin each writing session with a TQW lesson. The lessons take from 5 to 20 minutes. Most run about 10 or 15 minutes. This will leave the students with a 25–30 minute block of writing time and will give them the chance to bring the idea you've taught into their own writing. If your schedule doesn't allow students to write three days a week, we recommend you find stretches in the school year when they can. Rather than have students write one or two days a week all year long, look for six-week stretches when you can build in three sessions a week, cutting back at other times to a lighter schedule.

Learning to write, like any other complex skill, requires lots of practice. Don't be surprised if student growth seems slow if time on task is limited. You wouldn't expect to learn to play the piano or tennis with limited practice time regardless of how much teaching was going on.

The TQW lessons can be used for whole-class instruction or for working with a targeted small group. In fact, you may find an individual lesson that offers just the advice a single writer may need. As you become familiar with the lessons, you may find yourself bringing the information into your one-on-one conferences with students.

For more on scheduling and ways to organize your classroom for writing time, see *Writing Workshop: The Essential Guide*, by Ralph Fletcher and JoAnn Portalupi.

References

Cary, Stephen. (2000). *Working with
Second Language Learners: Answers to Teacher's
Top Ten Questions.* Portsmouth, New Hampshire:
Heinemann.

Fletcher, Ralph and JoAnn Portalupi. (2001).
Writing Workshop: The Essential Guide.
Portsmouth, New Hampshire: Heinemann.

Krashen, Stephen and Tracy Terrell. (1983).
*The Natural Approach: Language Acquisition in
the Classroom.* Oxford: Pergamon Press.

Murray, Donald. (1982). *Learning by Teaching:
Selected Articles on Writing and Teaching.*
Portsmouth, New Hampshire: Boynton/Cook-
Heinemann.

Noden, Harry. (1999). *Image Grammar:
Using Grammatical Structures to Teach Writing.*
Portsmouth, New Hampshire: Heinemann.

Zinsser, William. (2001). *On Writing Well:
An Informal Guide to Writing Nonfiction.*
New York: Harper Collins Publishers.

Appendix A: The Writer's Lifeblood

I write when I'm inspired—and I see to it that I'm inspired every morning at 9 a.m.

— *Amos Oz*

People want to know why I do this, why I write such gross stuff. I like to tell them I have the heart of a small boy—and I keep it in a jar on my desk.

— *Stephen King*

I know nothing about the technical stuff of writing, like where to put a comma. What I know about writing has to do with where you put your heart.

— *Nasdijj, The Blood Runs Like a River Through My Dreams*

The adjective is the enemy of the noun.

— *Voltaire*

My task is to make you hear, to make you feel—and, above all, to make you see. That is all, and it is everything.

— *Joseph Conrad*

The secret wish of poetry is to stop time.

— *Charles Simic*

Writing a poem is like giving blood. It goes straight from the heart of the writer to the heart of the reader.

— *Ralph Fletcher*

The three worst pieces of advice I've been given:
1. If you like it, cut it out.
2. Know what you are going to say before you write it.
3. That's been said before.

— *Don Murray*

Imagine yourself at your kitchen table, in your pajamas. Imagine one person you'd allow to see you that way, and write in the voice you'd use to that friend.

— *Sandra Cisneros*

Write about what makes you different.

— *Sandra Cisneros*

The basic law is B.I.C. (Butt In Chair).

— *Ann Lamott*

Nina dies sine linea (Never a day without a line).

— *Horace*

I write for two hours a day, but it's what I do for the other twenty-two hours that allows me to do that writing.

— *Don Murray*

Inside every fat book is a thin book trying to get out.

— *Unknown*

Tell me, what is it you plan to do with your one wild and precious life?

— *Mary Oliver*

I know a poem is finished when I can't find another word to cut.

– *Bobbi Katz*

Writing stories has given me the power to change things I could not change as a child. I can make boys into doctors. I can make fathers stop drinking. I can make mothers stay.

– *Cynthia Rylant*

Don't say the old lady screamed. Bring her on and let her scream.

– *Mark Twain*

The beautiful part of writing is that you don't have to get it right the first time, unlike, say, a brain surgeon. You can always do it better, find the exact word, the apt phrase, the leaping simile.

– *Robert Cormier*

I think of writing as a way of seeing. It's a way of bringing out the specialness of ordinary things.

– *Laurence Yep*

Today is fair. Tomorrow may be overcast with clouds. My words are like the stars that never change.

– *Chief Seattle*

In baseball you get three strikes and you're out. In writing you get as many whacks at the ball as you want until you finally get a hit.

– *Tomie dePaola*

I seek words, I chase after them. When I write I'm trying to put the most beautiful words in the world down on paper.

– *Cynthia Rylant*

Keep listening. Keep your radar out. Take everything, because it is matter for your work. No detail is too small.

– *Mary Tallmountain*

A writer should know how much change a character has in his pockets.

– *James Joyce*

If I write what you know, I bore you; if I write what I know; I bore myself, there I write what I don't know.

– *Robert Duncan*

Poems are fire for the cold, ropes let down to the lost, something as necessary as bread in the pockets of the hungry.

– *Mary Oliver*

I don't create characters so much as I make room inside my mind and heart for them to come and get me. I am drawn to characters who make me feel deeply—make me mad, confuse me, make me wonder, break my heart, stagger me with what they are up against.

– *Carolyn Coman*

Appendix B:

- **Authors' tea:**
  students share selected work as they celebrate with refreshments.

- **Bulletin boards:**
  nonfiction writing can accompany photos, charts, maps, and other print-related materials to teach a theme.

- **Chap books:**
  small collections of one writer's poetry—themed or unthemed.

- **Class anthology:**
  a collection of the students' writing, themed or unthemed.

- **Events:**
  look for the purposeful writing associated with events: invitations, advertisements, synopsis, background information.

- **Explanatory text posted next to projects or museum exhibit:**
  museum viewers look to the side of a painting or artifact to read about its history. Don't forget to include this writing in student displays.

- **Feature article:**
  publish special topic feature articles in class, school, or local newspapers.

- **Hosting storytime lunch or snack:**
  regularly scheduled story times where students can sign up to share their work with others.

- **Information brochure:**
  publish student information writing in this tri-fold format and make it available in an authentic context as topic demands.

- **Multi genre research project:**
  students research a topic and use the information to produce writing in many different genres.

- **Oral report or debate:**
  note taking, opening and closing arguments, and summaries of main points all contribute to successful oral events.

- **Poem-in-a-pocket:**
  students publish their work on pocket-size cards. Build a classroom collection from which students choose. Students select a poem to carry in their pocket for a day, sharing and reading as they desire.

- **Poetry jams:**
  reciting aloud one's work to a larger audience who show appreciation by snapping fingers instead of clapping.

- **Published poems tucked in the covers of books:**
  students pair their published poems with novels or picture books and slip them into the jackets of the books. A note to the reader from the poet can explain the connection the poem has to the book.

- **Recitations:**
  learning a poem by heart can be a powerful experience. Don't forget to have fun designing choral readings of favorite poems.

- **School-wide authors' day:**
  students from classrooms across school celebrate their writing on a designated day. This may include reading in large or small cross-grade groupins; opening the school to parents, grandparents, community members, inviting visiting authors to participate.

- **Story shelf in classroom library:**
  encourage students to read each other's work by making it available among other published texts.

- **Student-authored books donated to local doctors' offices waiting rooms:**
  look for places where student writing will be appreciated.

- **Teaching poster:**
  research writing designed in a poster format and hung to teach others.

- **Visit to another class:**
  visiting authors arrive to read their work (akin to traveling minstrels).

- **Visiting author's get-together:**
  authors' tea by another name.

- **Visiting poets:**
  invite another poet—of any age—to read or recite their work to the class.

- **Wall posters:**
  short texts enlarged and posted for easy, frequent, repeated readings.

Book Title	Author	Publisher	ISBN	Lesson Title	Quality
A Chair for My Mother	Vera B. Williams	Mulberry	0688040748	Control How Time Moves	Design
A Medieval Feast	Aliki	HarperTrophy	0064460509	Use Authentic Details	Ideas
All About Owls	Jim Arnosky	Scholastic	043905852X	Lead with a Question	Design
All About Rattlesnakes	Jim Arnosky	Scholastic	0439376173	Lead with a Question	Design
Anansi the Spider	Gerald McDermott	Henry Holt & Company	0805003118	Try a New Genre	Ideas
Annie Rose is My Little Sister	Shirley Hughes	Candlewick Press	0763619590	Use a Snapshot Structure	Design
Are You a Snail?	Judy Allen and Tudor Humphries	Larousse Kingfisher Chambers	0753452421	Capture the Power of One	Design
Beaver at Long Pond	William T. George	Greenwillow	0688071066	Capture the Power of One	Design
Because of Winn-Dixie	Kate Dicamillo	Candlewick	0763616052	Write in the First Person	Ideas
Before I Was Your Mother	Karen Lasky	Harcourt Children's Books	0152014640	Use a Snapshot Structure	Design
Birthday Presents	Cynthia Rylant	Orchard Books	0531070263	Use a Symmetrical Design	Design
				Use a Thematic Focus	Design
				Write in the Second Person	Ideas
				Use a Snapshot Structure	Design
Bitter Bananas	Isaac Olaleye	Puffin	0140557105	Create Suspense in Fiction	Design
Box Turtle at Long Pond	William T. George	Greenwillow	0688081843	Capture the Power of One	Design
Brave Irene	William Steig	Farrar, Straus, & Giroux	0374409277	Work with an External Conflict	Ideas
				Write in the Third Person	Ideas
				Use Plot, Place, and Character in a Story	Ideas
				Use Personification	Ideas
				Use Details to Bring Alive a Setting	Ideas
Charlie Anderson	Barbara Abercrombie	Aladdin Library	0689801149	Write in Third Person	Ideas
Charlotte's Web	E. B. White	HarperTrophy	0064400557	Try a New Genre	Ideas
Chato's Kitchen	Gary Soto	Putnam	0399226583	Use Choice Adjectives	Language
Chrysanthemum	Kevin Henkes	HarperTrophy	0688147321	Write in the Third Person	Ideas
Come on, Rain!	Karen Hesse	Scholastic	0590331256	Use Choice Adjectives	Language
Crab Moon	Ruth Horowitz	Candlewick Press	0763607096	Use General Info. and Specific Details	Ideas
Crane Wife, The	Odds Bodkin	Harcourt	0152163506	Create Suspense in Fiction	Design
Dogs	Seymour Simon	HarperCollins	0060289430	Try a New Genre	Ideas
Dogs Rule!	Daniel Kirk	Hyperion	0786819499	Try a New Genre	Ideas

Book Title	Author	Publisher	ISBN	Lesson Title	Quality
Dove Isabeau	Jane Yolen	Harcourt	0152015051	*Write in the Third Person*	**Ideas**
Dream Weaver	Johnathan London	SilverWhistle	0152009442	*Use Fresh Language*	**Language**
				Write in the Second Person	**Ideas**
Every Living Thing	Cynthia Rylant	Aladdin	0689712634	*Try a New Genre*	**Ideas**
Fig Pudding	Ralph Fletcher	Dell Yearling	044041203X	*End with Humor*	**Design**
Fly Away Home	Eve Bunting	Clarion Books	0395664152	*Work with an External Conflict*	**Ideas**
				Use Plot, Place, and Character in a Story	**Ideas**
Flying Solo	Ralph Fletcher	Yearling Books	0440416019	*Organize Your Writing*	**Design**
Forest, The	Claire Nivola	Farrar, Straus & Giroux	0374324522	*Work with an External Confilct*	**Ideas**
Fox	Margaret Wild	Kane/Miller Book Pub.	1929132166	*Develop Your Characters*	**Ideas**
				Use Details to Bring Alive a Setting	**Ideas**
				Work with an Internal Conflict	**Ideas**
				Use Plot, Place, and Character in a Story	**Ideas**
				Move from Simple to Complex Sentences	**Language**
				Use Verbs That Describe Action	**Language**
Gardener, The	Sarah Stewart	Farrar, Straus, & Giroux	0374325170	*Create Illustrations for the Text*	**Presentation**
				Use Plot, Place, and Character in a Story	**Ideas**
Ghost-Eye Tree	Bill Martin, Jr.	Henry Holt & Company	0805002081	*Write a Circular Story*	**Design**
Gila Monsters Meet You at the Airport	Marjorie Sharmat	Scott Foresman	0689713835	*Elaborate on an Idea*	**Ideas**
Girl Wonder: A Baseball Story in Nine Innings	Deborah Hopkinson	Atheneum	0689833008	*Organize Your Writing*	**Design**
Hatchet	Gary Paulsen	Simon Pulse	0689826990	*Use Plot, Place, and Character in a Story*	**Ideas**
Hello, Harvest Moon	Ralph Fletcher	Clarion Books	0618164510	*Write in Second Person*	**Ideas**
				Elaborate on an Idea	**Ideas**
Holes	Louis Sacher	Yearling	0440414806	*Use Details to Bring the Setting Alive*	**Ideas**
Honest-to-Goodness Truth, The	Patricia McKissack	Anthenum	0689826680	*Work with an Internal Conflict*	**Ideas**
I Live in Tokyo	Mari Takabayashi	Houghton Mifflin	0618007022	*Use Natural Voice*	**Language**
Ira Sleeps Over	Bernard Weber	Houghton Mifflin	0395205034	*Use a Triangular Structure*	**Design**
Joey Pigza Swallowed the Key	Jack Gantos	HarperTrophy	0064408337	*Write in the First Person*	**Ideas**

Book Title	Author	Publisher	ISBN	Lesson Title	Quality
Julie of the Wolves	Jean Craighead George	HarperTrophy	0064400581	*Describe What Your Character Looks Like*	**Ideas**
Julius, the Baby of the World	Kevin Henkes	HarperTrophy	0688143881	*Work with an External Conflict*	**Ideas**
Knots on a Counting Rope	Bill Martin, Jr.	Owlet	0805029559	*Use Inference to Let Readers to Fill in the Gap*	**Ideas**
Learning to Swim in Swaziland	Nila K. Leigh	Scholastic	0590459384	*Use a Natural Voice*	**Language**
Louis the Fish	Arthur Yorinks	Farrar, Straus, & Giroux	0374445982	*End with Humor*	**Design**
Moon and You, The	E. C. Krupp	HarperCollins	0688178189	*Make a Comparison*	**Ideas**
Morning, Noon, and Night	Jean Craighead George	Scholastic	0493285070	*Use Subtitles to Organize Your Writing*	**Design**
Mud	Mary Lyn Ray	Voyager Books	0015202461	*Choose Words That Sound Like What They Mean*	**Language**
				Use Alliteration	**Language**
Mud Is Cake	Pam Muñoz Ryan	Hyperion Press	0786805013	*Elaborate on an Idea*	**Ideas**
My Rotten Redhead Older Brother	Patricia Polacco	Aladdin Library	0689820364	*Work with an External Conflict*	**Ideas**
Night in the Country	Cynthia Rylant	Aladdin Library	0689714734	*Vary The Length of Sentences*	**Language**
No, David	David Shannon	Scholastic	842418114X	*Create Ilustrations for the Text*	**Presentation**
Now One Foot, Now the Other	Tomie de Paola	Putnam Juvenile	0399207759	*Use a Symmetrical Design*	**Design**
Officer Buckle and Gloria	Peggy Rathman	Weston Woods Studios	0788206699	*Create Ilustrations for the Text*	**Presentation**
Other Side, The	Jacqueline Woodson	Putnam Publishing Group	0399231161	*Come Up with the Right Ending*	**Design**
Out of the Dust	Karen Hesse	Scholastic	0590371258	*Describe What Your Character Looks Like*	**Ideas**
Owl Moon	Jane Yolen	Philomel Books	0399214577	*Control How Time Moves*	**Design**
				Use Fresh Language	**Language**
				Use a Time Focus	**Design**
Ox-Cart Man, The	Donald Hall	Puffin	0140504419	*Use Authentic Details*	**Idea**
Pain and the Great One, The	Judy Blume	Dragonfly	0440409675	*Elaborate on an Idea*	**Ideas**
				Use a Symmetrical Design	**Design**
Paper Bag Princess, The	Robert Munsch	Annick	0920236162	*Come Up with the Right Ending*	**Design**
Paperboy	Dav Pilkey	Orchard Books	0531071391	*Use a Time Focus*	**Design**
				Create Illustrations for Text	**Presentation**

Book Title	Author	Publisher	ISBN	Lesson Title	Quality
Pete's a Pizza	William Steig	HarperFestival	0062051571	*Use Parentheses to Add Information*	**Presentation**
				Use a Time Focus	**Design**
Poems from Where the Sidewalk Ends	Shel Silverstein	HarperCollins	0060256672	*End with Humor*	**Design**
Raft, The	Jim LaMarche	HarperCollins	0688139779	*Use Alliteration*	**Language**
Relatives Came, The	Cynthia Rylant	Pearson Learning	0689717385	*Use a Circular Story*	**Design**
				Use a Symmetrical Design	**Design**
Roller Coaster	Marla Freeze	Harcourt Children's Books	0152045546	*Use a Triangular Structure*	**Design**
Scarecrow	Cynthia Rylant	Voyager Books	0152024808	*Use General Information and Specific Details*	**Ideas**
Sheila Rae, the Brave	Kevin Henkes	Scholastic	059046406X	*Use a Symmetrical Design*	**Design**
Shrek!	William Steig	Sunburst	0374466238	*Write in the Third Person*	**Ideas**
Spider Boy	Ralph Fletcher	Yearling Books	0440414830	*Try a New Genre*	**Ideas**
Summer My Father Was Ten, The	Pat Brisson	Boyd Mills Press	1563978296	*Work with an Internal Conflict*	**Ideas**
Sylvester and the Magic Pebble	William Steig	Prentice Hall	0671662694	*Use a Triangular Structure*	**Design**
True Story of the Three Little Pigs, The	Jon Sciezka	Dutton Books	0140540563	*Write in the First Person*	**Ideas**
Twilight Comes Twice	Ralph Fletcher	Houghton Mifflin	0395848261	*Elaborate on an Idea*	**Ideas**
				Use a Symmetrical Design	**Design**
Two of Them, The	Aliki	William Morrow	0688073379	*Lead with the Big Picture*	**Design**
				Use a Recurring Detail	**Design**
Uncle Daddy	Ralph Fletcher	Henry Holt & Company	0805066632	*Write in the First Person*	**Ideas**
Verdi	Janell Cannon	Harcourt	0152010289	*Develop Your Characters*	**Ideas**
Very Last First Time	Jan Andrews	Groundwood	088899043X	*Use Details to Bring the Setting Alive*	**Ideas**
War with Grandpa, The	Robert Kimmel Smith	Yearling Books	0440492769	*Work with an External Conflict*	**Ideas**
When I Was Nine	James Stevenson	William Morrow	0688059430	*Use a Snapshot Structure*	**Design**
When I Was Young in the Mountains	Cynthia Rylant	Puffin	0140548750	*Use a Snapshot Structure*	**Design**
When Sophie Got Angry — Really, Really Angry	Molly Bang	Scholastic	0590189794	*Create Illustrations for the Text*	**Presentation**

Appendix D:
A Blank Road Map for Use

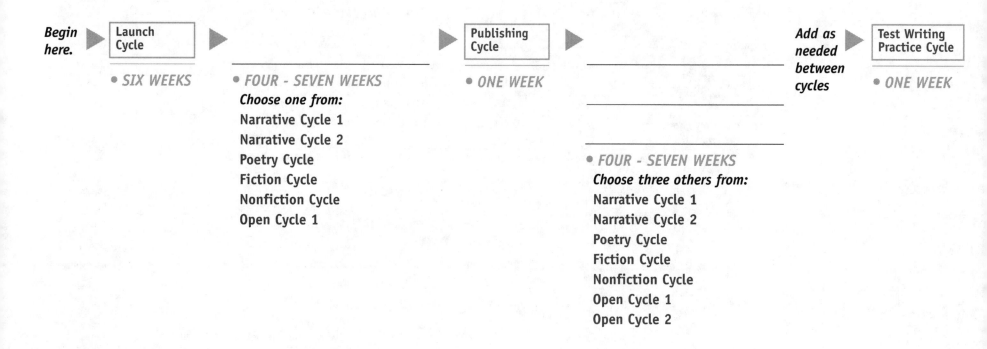

Begin here. ▶ | Launch Cycle | ▶

* SIX WEEKS

_____

* FOUR - SEVEN WEEKS
Choose one from:
Narrative Cycle 1
Narrative Cycle 2
Poetry Cycle
Fiction Cycle
Nonfiction Cycle
Open Cycle 1

▶ | Publishing Cycle | ▶

* ONE WEEK

_____

_____

* FOUR - SEVEN WEEKS
Choose three others from:
Narrative Cycle 1
Narrative Cycle 2
Poetry Cycle
Fiction Cycle
Nonfiction Cycle
Open Cycle 1
Open Cycle 2

Add as needed between cycles ▶ | Test Writing Practice Cycle |

* ONE WEEK

Possible Yearly Road Maps

First Year Possible Road Map

Begin here. ▶ Launch Cycle ▶ Open Cycle 1 ▶ Publishing Cycle ▶ Narrative Cycle 1 ▶ Test Writing Practice Cycle ▶ Open Cycle 2 ▶ Test Writing Practice Cycle ▶ Poetry Cycle

• SIX WEEKS • FOUR WEEKS • ONE WEEK • SIX WEEKS • ONE WEEK • FOUR WEEKS • ONE WEEK • FIVE WEEKS

Second Year Possible Road Map

Begin here. ▶ Launch Cycle ▶ Open Cycle 1 ▶ Publishing Cycle ▶ Test Writing Practice Cycle ▶ Narrative Cycle 2 ▶ Open Cycle 2 ▶ Test Writing Practice Cycle ▶ Nonfiction Cycle

• SIX WEEKS • FOUR WEEKS • ONE WEEK • ONE WEEK • SIX WEEKS • FOUR WEEKS • ONE WEEK • FIVE WEEKS

Third Year Possible Road Map

Begin here. ▶ Open Cycle 1 ▶ Publishing Cycle ▶ Fiction Cycle ▶ Test Writing Practice Cycle ▶ Open Cycle 2 ▶ Test Writing Practice Cycle ▶ Poetry Cycle ▶ Nonfiction Cycle

• FOUR WEEKS • ONE WEEK • SEVEN WEEKS • ONE WEEK • FOUR WEEKS • ONE WEEK • FIVE WEEKS • FIVE WEEKS

Fourth Year Possible Road Map

Begin here. ▶ Open Cycle 1 ▶ Publishing Cycle ▶ Narrative Cycle 2 ▶ Test Writing Practice Cycle ▶ Open Cycle 2 ▶ Test Writing Practice Cycle ▶ Nonfiction Cycle ▶ Fiction Cycle

• FOUR WEEKS • ONE WEEK • SIX WEEKS • ONE WEEK • FOUR WEEKS • ONE WEEK • FIVE WEEKS • SEVEN WEEKS

Teacher Assessment Form

Student _____ Date _____

	Strengths	Areas to Grow	Lessons/Strategies
Ideas			
Design			
Language			
Presentation			

End of Cycle Assessment — Launch

Student	Ideas	Design	Language	Presentation
	Is getting comfortable writing. Sees his/her life as a good source for writing ideas. Uses supporting details.	Focuses a story around a main idea (theme). Focuses a story around a specific event (time.)	Uses lively verbs. Uses precise nouns. Uses descriptive adjectives.	Begins to use an editing checklist to find errors. Finds and corrects spelling errors.

End of Cycle Assessment — Narrative 1

Student	Ideas	Design	Language	Presentations
	Shows evidence of plot, setting, and characters. Uses details to flesh out plot, setting, and characters.	Uses leads and endings that are lively and effective. Uses details to create and develop a scene. Organizes writing so the reader can follow it.	Writes with an original voice. Uses fresh language in sentences.	Uses a variety of sentence beginnings. Uses the consistent tense of verbs. Breaks long texts in paragraphs.

End of Cycle Assessment — Narrative 2

Student	Ideas	Design	Language	Presentation
	Clearly defines plot, place, and character Uses details to effectively describe settings or characters.	Writes clearly focused narratives. Writes leads and endings that show awareness of the reader. Organizes writing with attention to how events are communicated to reader. Effectively handles time in narrative.	Writes with a distinctive voice (unique to the student). Sometimes uses repetition in story.	Uses a variety of punctuation that allows for interesting and complex sentence structure. Edits for passive voice. Experiments with the colon or semi-colon.

End of Cycle Assessment — Poetry

Student	Ideas	Design	Language	Presentation
	Builds poems on the foundation of a strong image, emotion, and/or music. Uses a range of sensory details. Uses poetic devices (metaphor, personification) to express ideas.	Focuses a poem. Writes poems with a clear sense of closure. Uses white space and line breaks to reinforce meaning.	Attends to the sounds of words. Uses repetition. Uses a Thesaurus to select the precise word.	Displays an economy of language that leaves the poem free of clutter. Finds and removes cliches or other weak parts.

End of Cycle Assessment — Fiction

Student	Ideas	Design	Language	Presentation
	Establishes an external or internal conflict. Embellishes a true story. Experiments with different points of view. Uses details to create suspense in a story.	Experiments with various story shapes (triangular, snapshot, circular). Deliberately crafts a lead to hook the reader. Paces stories by carefully attending to the element of time.	Writes a flow/rhythm that supports the events of the story.	Edits so a story can be read by other people. Experiments with writing both short and long sentences.

End of Cycle Assessment — Nonfiction

Student	Ideas	Design	Language	Presentation
	Displays knowledge/authority on the subject. Uses authentic details to make the writing engaging to read.	Has a focus for the subject. Uses clear organization that makes it easy to follow. Has the right distance from the topic.	Writes in a natural voice about nonfiction topics. Integrates specialized vocabulary into the writing. Makes comparisons that acknowledge a reader's experience.	Edits with a concern for the reader. Uses commas to list ideas.

End of Cycle Assessment — Open Cycle

	Ideas	Design	Language	Presentation
Student				

Daily Record-keeping Form

Date _____

Lesson	
Exemplar Texts	
Conference Notes	
Notes for Future Lessons	

Week-at-a-Glance Record-keeping Form

	Monday	Tuesday	Wednesday	Thursday	Friday
Lesson					
Exemplar Text					
Conference Notes					
Future Plans					

Cycle-at-a-Glance — Launch

Date	Lesson Identifier	Lesson	Notes
	I-4	*Dig Up Buried Stories*	
	I-1	*Create an Authority List*	
	I-12	*Free-Write for Specifics*	
	D-30	*Find Your Focus*	
	I-17	*Use Supporting Details*	
	D-15	*Use a Thematic Focus*	
	D-16	*Use a Time Focus*	
	L-23	*Use Verbs That Describe Action*	
	L-22	*Use Precise Nouns*	
	L-21	*Use Choice Adjectives*	
	P-10	*Edit with a Checklist*	
	P-8	*Be Aware of Words You Commonly Misspell*	
	P-11	*Fix Spelling Errors*	

Cycle-at-a-Glance — Narrative 1

Date	Lesson Identifier	Lesson	Notes
	I-8	*Use Plot, Place, and Character in a Story*	
	I-22 *or* I-25	*Bring Your Characters to Life* *or* *Develop Your Characters*	
	I-23	*Describe What Your Characters Look Like*	
	I-24	*Develop the Inner Story*	
	I-27	*Use Details to Bring the Setting Alive*	
	D-3	*Organize Your Writing*	
	D-21	*Write a Lively Lead*	
	D-22	*Write a Waterfall Lead*	
	D-23	*Come Up with the Right Ending*	
	I-15	*Use General Information and Specific Details*	
	L-9	*Use Fresh Language*	
	P-5	*Use Parentheses to Add Information*	
	D-29	*Develop a Scene*	
	L-19	*Write Believable Dialogue*	
	P-14	*Break a Text into Paragraphs*	
	L-13	*Vary Sentence Beginnings*	
	P-15	*Stop the Run-on Sentence*	
	P-16	*Use Consistent Tense*	

Cycle-at-a-Glance — Narrative 2

Date	Lesson Identifier	Lesson	Notes
	I-8	*Use Plot, Place, and Character in a Story*	
	D-13	*Use a Double Focus in a Narrative*	
	D-31	*Use Details to Alter the Pace of Time*	
	D-4	*Use a Recurring Detail*	
	D-33	*Use a Symmetrical Design*	
	D-7	*Use 2-3-1 Format for Organization*	
	D	*Choose one of the lessons on Leads* **D-17, D-18, D-19, D-20, D-21, D-22**	
	D	*Choose one of the lessons on Endings* **D-23, D-24, D-25, D-26**	
	L-17	*Tighten Dialogue*	
	I-13	*Invent Specifics to Fill In Memory Gaps*	
	I-16	*Use Inference to Let Readers Fill In the Gap*	
	L-12	*Move From Simple to Complex Sentences*	
	L-7	*Use Repetition in Narrative Writing*	
	P-3 *or* P-6	*Use Commas to Add an Aside* *or* *Use the Dash to Spotlight Part of a Sentence*	
	P-1 *or* P-2	*Use a Colon to Introduce a List or Idea* *or* *Use a Semicolon to Pull Together Related Sentences*	
	L-2	*Avoid Redundant Words*	
	L-1	*Avoid Confusing Pronouns*	
	P-9	*Edit for Passive Voice*	

Cycle-at-a-Glance — Poetry

Date	Lesson Identifier	Lesson	Notes
	I-3	*Create a Poem with Imagery, Emotion, and Music*	
	I-2	*Create a Poem from a Story*	
	I-20	*Use a Metaphor*	
	D-14	*Use a Double Focus in a Poem*	
	L-6	*Create Line Breaks in a Poem*	
	L-10	*Use Repetition in Poetry*	
	L-8	*Use Alliteration*	
	L-5	*Choose Words That Sound Like What They Mean*	
	L-20	*Use a Thesaurus to Find Just the Right Word*	
	D-26	*End with Your Strongest Line*	
	D-8	*Use White Space in a Poem*	
	I-21	*Use Personification*	
	P-17	*Use Fragments When You Write a Poem*	
	L-3	*Delete the Weak Parts*	
	L-15	*Avoid Clichés*	

Cycle-at-a-Glance — Fiction

Date	Lesson Identifier	Lesson	Notes
	I-8	*Use Plot, Place, and Character in a Story*	
	I-11	*Embellish an Idea*	
	I-28	*Work with an External Conflict*	
	I-29	*Work with an Internal Conflict*	
	I-18	*Value Your Experience*	
	I-26	*Make Your Story Believable*	
	I-30	*Write in the First Person*	
	I-31	*Write in the Second Person*	
	I-32	*Write in the Third Person*	
	D-28	*Create Suspense in Fiction*	
	D-27	*Control How Time Moves*	
	D-34	*Use a Triangular Structure*	
	D-32	*Use a Snapshot Structure*	
	D-35	*Write a Circular Story or Poem*	
	D-17	*Cut to Your Lead*	
	D19	*Lead with the Big Picture*	
	D	*Choose one of the lessons on Endings* **D-23, D-24, D-25, D-26**	
	L-4	*Remove Those Annoying Little Qualifiers*	
	L-11	*Combine Short Sentences*	
	L-14	*Vary the Length of Sentences*	

Cycle-at-a-Glance —Nonfiction

Date	Lesson Identifier	Lesson	Notes
	L-18	*Use a Natural Voice*	
	D-10	*Find the Right Distance by Pulling in Close*	
	D-11	*Find the Right Distance by Pulling Back*	
	D-1	*Anticipate What the Audience Expects*	
	D-9	*Capture the Power of One*	
	I-14	*Use Authentic Details*	
	D-6	*Use Subtitles to Organize Your Writing*	
	D-20	*Open with a Scene*	
	D-18	*Lead with a Question*	
	L-24	*Use Vocabulary Specific to a Subject*	
	D-5	*Use a Transition Between Ideas*	
	I-19	*Make a Comparison*	
	P-4	*Use Commas to List Ideas*	
	P-7	*Use the Ellipsis*	
	L-16	*Avoid Passive Verbs*	

Cycle-at-a-Glance — Launch

I-4 *Dig Up Buried Stories*	**I-1** *Create an Authority List*	**I-12** *Free-Write for Specifics*	**D-30** *Find Your Focus*	**I-17** *Use Supporting Details*
D-15 *Use a Thematic Focus*	**D-16** *Use a Time Focus*	**L-23** *Use Verbs That Describe Action*	**L-22** *Use Precise Nouns*	**L-21** *Use Choice Adjectives*
P-10 *Edit with a Checklist*	**P-8** *Be Aware of Words You Commonly Misspell*	**P-11** *Fix Spelling Errors*		

Cycle-at-a-Glance — Narrative 1

I-8 *Use Plot, Place, and Character in a Story*

I-22 *Bring Your Characters to Life*

I-25 *Develop Your Characters*

I-23 *Describe What Your Characters Look Like*

I-24 *Develop the Inner Story*

I-27 *Use Details to Bring the Setting Alive*

D-3 *Organize Your Writing*

D-21 *Write a Lively Lead*

D-22 *Write a Waterfall Lead*

D-23 *Come Up with the Right Ending*

I-15 *Use General Information and Specific Details*

L-9 *Use Fresh Language*

P-5 *Use Parentheses to Add Information*

D-29 *Develop a Scene*

L-19 *Write Believable Dialogue*

P-14 *Break a Text into Paragraphs*

L-13 *Vary Sentence Beginnings*

P-15 *Stop the Run-on Sentence*

P-16 *Use Consistent Tense*

Cycle-at-a-Glance — Narrative 2

I-8 *Use Plot, Place, and Character in a Story*	**D-13** *Use a Double Focus in a Narrative*	**D-31** *Use Details to Alter the Pace of Time*	**D-4** *Use a Recurring Detail*	**D-33** *Use a Symmetrical Design*
D-7 *Use 2-3-1 Format for Organization*	*Choose one of the lessons on Leads* **D-17, D-18, D-19, D-20, D-21, D-22**	*Choose one of the lessons on Endings* **D-23, D-24, D-25, D-26**	**L-17** *Tighten Dialogue*	**I-13** *Invent Specifics to Fill In Memory Gaps*
I-16 *Use Inference to Let Readers Fill In the Gap*	**L-12** *Move From Simple to Complex Sentences*	**L-7** *Try Repetition in Narrative Writing*	**P-3** *Use Commas to Add an Aside*	**P-6** *Use the Dash to Spotlight Part of a Sentence*
P-1 *Use a Colon to Introduce a List or Idea*	**P-2** *Use a Semicolon to Pull Together Related Sentences*	**L-2** *Avoid Redundant Words*	**L-1** *Avoid Confusing Pronouns*	**P-9** *Edit for Passive Voice*

Cycle-at-a-Glance — Poetry

I-3 *Create a Poem with Imagery, Emotion, and Music*	**I-2** *Create a Poem from a Story*	**I-20** *Use a Metaphor*	**D-14** *Use a Double Focus in a Poem*	**L-6** *Create Line Breaks in a Poem*
L-10 *Use Repetition in Poetry*	**L-8** *Use Alliteration*	**L-5** *Choose Words That Sound Like What They Mean*	**L-20** *Use a Thesaurus to Find Just the Right Word*	**D-26** *End with Your Strongest Line*
D-8 *Use White Space in a Poem*	**I-21** *Use Personification*	**P-17** *Use Fragments When You Write a Poem*	**L-3** *Delete the Weak Parts*	**L-15** *Avoid Clichés*

Cycle-at-a-Glance — Fiction

I-8 *Use Plot, Place, and Character in a Story*	**I-11** *Embellish an Idea*	**I-28** *Work with an External Conflict*	**I-29** *Work with an Internal Conflict*	**I-18** *Value Your Experience*
I-26 *Make Your Story Believable*	**I-30** *Write in the First Person*	**I-31** *Write in the Second Person*	**I-32** *Write in the Third Person*	**D-28** *Create Suspense in Fiction*
D-27 *Control How Time Moves*	**D-34** *Use a Triangular Structure*	**D-32** *Use a Snapshot Structure*	**D-35** *Write a Circular Story or Poem*	**D-17** *Cut to Your Lead*
D19 *Lead with the Big Picture*	*Choose one of the lessons on Endings* **D-23, D-24, D-25, D-26**	**L-4** *Remove Those Annoying Little Qualifiers*	**L-11** *Combine Short Sentences*	**L-14** *Vary the Length of Sentences*

Cycle-at-a-Glance — Nonfiction

L-18 *Use a Natural Voice*	**D-10** *Find the Right Distance by Pulling in Close*	**D-11** *Find the Right Distance by Pulling Back*	**D-1** *Anticipate What the Audience Expects*	**D-9** *Capture the Power of One*
I-14 *Use Authentic Details*	**D-6** *Use Subtitles to Organize Your Writing*	**D-20** *Open with a Scene*	**D-18** *Lead with a Question*	**L-24** *Use Vocabulary Specific to a Subject*
D-5 *Use a Transition Between Ideas*	**I-19** *Make a Comparison*	**P-4** *Use Commas to List Ideas*	**P-7** *Use the Ellipsis*	**L-16** *Avoid Passive Verbs*

Conference Record Sheet — Launch

Student	Date	I-4 Dig Up Buried Stories	I-1 Create an Authority List	I-12 Free-Write for Specifics	D-30 Find Your Focus	I-17 Use Supporting Details	D-15 Use a Thematic Focus	D-16 Use a Time Focus	L-23 Use Verbs That Describe Action	L-22 Use Precise Nouns	L-21 Use Choice Adjectives	P-10 Edit with a Checklist	P-8 Be Aware of Words You Commonly Misspell	P-11 Fix Spelling Errors

Conference Record Sheet — Narrative 1

Student	Date	I-8 Use Plot, Place, and Character in a Story	I-22 Bring Your Characters to Life	I-25 Develop Your Characters	I-23 Describe What Your Characters Look Like	I-24 Develop the Inner Story	I-27 Use Details to Bring the Setting Alive	D-3 Organize Your Writing	D-21 Write a Lively Lead	D-22 Write a Waterfall Lead	D-23 Come Up with the Right Ending	I-15 Use General Information and Specific Details	L-9 Use Fresh Language	P-5 Use Parentheses to Add Information	D-29 Develop a Scene	L-19 Write Believable Dialogue	P-14 Break a Text into Paragraphs	L-13 Vary Sentence Beginnings	P-15 Stop the Run-on Sentence	P-16 Use Consistent Tense

Conference Record Sheet — Narrative 2

Student	Date	I-8 Use Plot, Place, and Character in a Story	D-13 Use a Double Focus in a Narrative	D-31 Use Details to Alter the Pace of Time	D-4 Use a Recurring Detail	D-33 Use a Symmetrical Design	D-7 Use 2-3-1 Format for Organization	Choose one of the lessons on Leads D-17, D-18, D-19, D-20, D-21, D-22	Choose one of the lessons on Endings D-23, D-24, D-25, D-26	L-17 Tighten Dialogue	I-13 Invent Specifics to Fill In Memory Gaps	I-16 Use Inference to Let Readers Fill In the Gap	L-12 Move From Simple to Complex Sentences	L-7 Try Repetition in Narrative Writing	P-3 Use Commas to Add an Aside	P-6 Use the Dash to Spotlight Part of a Sentence	P-1 Use a Colon to Introduce a List or Idea	P-2 Use a Semicolon to Pull Together Related Sentences	L-2 Avoid Redundant Words	L-1 Avoid Confusing Pronouns	P-9 Edit for Passive Voice

Conference Record Sheet — Poetry

Student	Date	I-3 Create a Poem with Imagery, Emotion, and Music	I-2 Create a Poem from a Story	I-20 Use a Metaphor	D-14 Use a Double Focus in a Poem	L-6 Create Line Breaks in a Poem	L-10 Use Repetition in Poetry	L-8 Use Alliteration	L-5 Choose Words That Sound Like What They Mean	L-20 Use a Thesaurus to Find Just the Right Word	D-26 End with Your Strongest Line	D-8 Use White Space in a Poem	I-21 Use Personification	P-17 Use Fragments When You Write a Poem	L-3 Delete the Weak Parts	L-15 Avoid Clichés

Conference Record Sheet — Fiction

Student	Date	I-8 Use Plot, Place, and Character in a Story	I-11 Embellish an Idea	I-28 Work with an External Conflict	I-29 Work with an Internal Conflict	I-18 Value Your Experience	I-26 Make Your Story Believable	I-30 Write in the First Person	I-31 Write in the Second Person	I-32 Write in the Third Person	D-28 Create Suspense in Fiction	D-27 Control How Time Moves	D-34 Use a Triangular Structure	D-32 Use a Snapshot Structure	D-35 Write a Circular Story or Poem	D-17 Cut to Your Lead	D19 Lead with the Big Picture	Choose one of the Lessons on Endings D-23, D-24, D-25, D-26	L-4 Remove Those Annoying Little Qualifiers	L-11 Combine Short Sentences	L-14 Vary the Length of Sentences

Conference Record Sheet — Nonfiction

Student	Date	**L-18** Use a Natural Voice	**D-10** Find the Right Distance by Pulling in Close	**D-11** Find the Right Distance by Pulling Back	**D-1** Anticipate What the Audience Expects	**D-9** Capture the Power of One	**I-14** Use Authentic Details	**D-6** Use Subtitles to Organize Your Writing	**D-20** Open with a Scene	**D-18** Lead with a Question	**L-24** Use Vocabulary Specific to a Subject	**D-5** Use a Transition Between Ideas	**I-19** Make a Comparison	**P-4** Use Commas to List Ideas	**P-7** Use the Ellipsis	**L-16** Avoid Passive Verbs

Conference Record Sheet — Open Cycle 1

Student	Date	I-17 Try a New Genre										

Conference Record Sheet — Open Cycle 2

Student	Date	I-5 Find Your Own Purpose for Writing										

Conference Record Sheet — Publishing

Student	Date	P-19 Choose What Gets Published	P-12 Personalize the Editing Checklist	P-18 Choose an Appropriate Form	P-20 Create Illustrations for the Text	P-21 Reflect on Your Writing

Conference Record Sheet — Test Writing Practice

Student	Date	I-19 Use R-U-P-R When Writing to a Prompt	I-10 Elaborate on an Idea	D-16 Make a Personal Connection	D-12 Stay on Topic	D-2 Include a Beginning, a Middle, and an End	P-13 Reread for Correctness

Conference Record Sheet — by date

Student	Date																	

Conference Chart

Uses of the Comma

Use	Example
Set off an "aside" from the main part of a sentence.	I reminded my friend, **who brought homemade brownies for lunch,** that he promised to trade with me today.

Personal Word List

Title _____   Name _____

Date _____

First Quarter	Second Quarter	Third Quarter	Fourth Quarter

Editing Checklist

Title _____   Name _____

Date _____

Skill	Student	Teacher
Sentence Sense		
Capital Letters		
Spelling		

Writing Reflection

Name _____   Date completed _____

Title_____   Cycle _____

Now that you're finished, take a minute to read and enjoy what you've written. Keep a record of what you're thinking today.

1) What are you particularly proud of in this piece of writing?

With the Process	**With the Product**

2) What would you like to improve upon?

With the Process	**With the Product**

Appendix F: Lesson List Arranged by Quality

Lesson Identifier	Quality *=Voice	Sub-Quality	IDEAS Lessons	Cycle†
	IDEAS			
I-1	I*	Topics	Create an Authority List	LC
I-2	I	Topics	Create a Poem from a Story	PC
I-3	I	Topics	Create a Poem with Imagery, Emotion, and Music	PC
I-4	I	Topics	Dig Up Buried Stories	LC
I-5	I	Topics	Find Your Own Purpose for Writing	OC2
I-6	I*	Topics	Make a Personal Connection	TWPC
I-7	I	Topics	Try a New Genre	OC2
I-8	I	Topics	Use Plot, Place, and Character in a Story	NC1
I-9	I	Topics	Use R-U-P-R When Writing to a Prompt	TWPC
I-10	I	Details	Elaborate on an Idea	TWPC
I-11	I	Details	Embellish an Idea	FC
I-12	I	Details	Free-Write for Specifics	LC
I-13	I	Details	Invent Specifics to Fill In Memory Gaps	NC2
I-14	I*	Details	Use Authentic Details	NFC
I-15	I	Details	Use General Information and Specific Details	NC1
I-16	I	Details	Use Inference to Let Readers Fill In the Gap	NC2
I-17	I	Details	Use Supporting Details	LC
I-18	I*	Details	Value Your Experience	FC
I-19	I	Compare/Contrast	Make a Comparison	NFC
I-20	I	Compare/Contrast	Use a Metaphor	PC
I-21	I	Compare/Contrast	Use Personification	PC
I-22	I*	Character/Setting	Bring Your Characters to Life	NC1
I-23	I	Character/Setting	Describe What Your Characters Look Like	NC1
I-24	I*	Character/Setting	Develop the Inner Story	NC1
I-25	I	Character/Setting	Develop Your Characters	NC1
I-26	I	Character/Setting	Make Your Story Believable	FC
I-27	I	Character/Setting	Use Details to Bring the Setting Alive	NC1
I-28	I	Character/Setting	Work with an External Conflict	FC
I-29	I*	Character/Setting	Work with an Internal Conflict	FC
I-30	I*	Point of View	Write in the First Person	FC
I-31	I*	Point of View	Write in the Second Person	FC
I-32	I*	Point of View	Write in the Third Person	FC

Lesson Identifier	Quality *=Voice	Sub-Quality	DESIGN Lessons	Cycle†
	DESIGN			
D-1	D	Organization	Anticipate What the Audience Expects	NFC
D-2	D	Organization	Include a Beginning, a Middle, and an End	TWPC
D-3	D	Organization	Organize Your Writing	NC1
D-4	D	Organization	Use a Recurring Detail	NC2
D-5	D	Organization	Use a Transition Between Ideas	NFC
D-6	D	Organization	Use Subtitles to Organize Your Writing	NFC
D-7	D	Organization	Use the 2-3-1 Format for Organization	NC2
D-8	D	Organization	Use White Space in a Poem	PC
D-9	D*	Focus	Capture the Power of One	NFC
D-10	D*	Focus	Find the Right Distance by Pulling in Close	NFC
D-11	D	Focus	Find the Right Distance by Pulling Back	NFC
D-12	D	Focus	Stay on Topic	TWPC
D-13	D	Focus	Use a Double Focus in a Narrative	NC2
D-14	D	Focus	Use a Double Focus in a Poem	PC
D-15	D*	Focus	Use a Thematic Focus	LC
D-16	D	Focus	Use a Time Focus	LC
D-17	D	Beginnings	Cut to Your Lead	FC
D-18	D*	Beginnings	Lead with a Question	NFC
D-19	D	Beginnings	Lead with the Big Picture	FC
D-20	D	Beginnings	Open with a Scene	NFC
D-21	D*	Beginnings	Write a Lively Lead	NC1
D-22	D	Beginnings	Write a Waterfall Lead	NC1
D-23	D	Endings	Come Up with the Right Ending	NC1
D-24	D	Endings	End with a Question	NC2
D-25	D*	Endings	End with Humor	NC2
D-26	D	Endings	End with Your Strongest Line	PC
D-27	D	Time	Control How Time Moves	FC
D-28	D	Time	Create Suspense in Fiction	FC
D-29	D	Time	Develop a Scene	NC1
D-30	D	Time	Find Your Focus	LC
D-31	D	Time	Use Details to Alter the Pace of Time	NC2
D-32	D	Shape	Use a Snapshot Structure	FC
D-33	D	Shape	Use a Symmetrical Design	NC2
D-34	D	Shape	Use a Triangular Structure	FC
D-35	D	Shape	Write a Circular Story or Poem	FC

Lesson List Arranged by Quality

Lesson Identifier	Quality *=Voice	Sub-Quality	LANGUAGE Lessons	Cycle†
		LANGUAGE		
L-1	L	Clarity	Avoid Confusing Pronouns	NC2
L-2	L	Clarity	Avoid Redundant Words	NC2
L-3	L	Clarity	Delete the Weak Parts	PC
L-4	L*	Clarity	Remove Those Annoying Little Qualifiers	FC
L-5	L	Music	Choose Words That Sound Like What They Mean	PC
L-6	L	Music	Create Line Breaks in a Poem	PC
L-7	L*	Music	Try Repetition in Narrative Writing	NC2
L-8	L	Music	Use Alliteration	PC
L-9	L	Music	Use Fresh Language	NC1
L-10	L	Music	Use Repetition in Poetry	PC
L-11	L	Sentences	Combine Short Sentences	FC
L-12	L	Sentences	Move From Simple to Complex Sentences	NC2
L-13	L	Sentences	Vary Sentence Beginnings	NC1
L-14	L*	Sentences	Vary the Length of Sentences	FC
L-15	L*	Voice	Avoid Clichés	PC
L-16	L	Voice	Avoid Passive Verbs	NFC
L-17	L	Voice	Tighten Dialogue	NC2
L-18	L*	Voice	Use a Natural Voice	NFC
L-19	L*	Voice	Write Believable Dialogue	NC1
L-20	L	Word Choice	Use a Thesaurus to Find Just the Right Word	PC
L-21	L	Word Choice	Use Choice Adjectives	LC
L-22	L	Word Choice	Use Precise Nouns	LC
L-23	L	Word Choice	Use Verbs That Describe Action	LC
L-24	L	Word Choice	Use Vocabulary Specific to a Subject	NFC

Lesson Identifier	Quality *=Voice	Sub-Quality	PRESENTATION Lessons	Cycle†
		PRESENTATION		
P-1	P	Cool Tools	Use a Colon to Introduce a List or Idea	NC2
P-2	P	Cool Tools	Use a Semicolon to Pull Together Related Sentences	NC2
P-3	P	Cool Tools	Use Commas to Add an Aside	NC2
P-4	P	Cool Tools	Use Commas to List Ideas	NFC
P-5	P*	Cool Tools	Use Parentheses to Add Information	NC1
P-6	P*	Cool Tools	Use the Dash to Spotlight Part of a Sentence	NC2
P-7	P	Cool Tools	Use the Ellipsis	NFC
P-8	P	Editing	Be Aware of Words You Commonly Misspell	LC
P-9	P*	Editing	Edit for Passive Voice	NC2
P-10	P	Editing	Edit with a Checklist	LC
P-11	P	Editing	Fix Spelling Errors	LC
P-12	P	Editing	Personalize the Editing Checklist	PUBC
P-13	P	Editing	Reread for Correctness	TWPC
P-14	P	Conventions	Break a Text into Paragraphs	NC1
P-15	P	Conventions	Stop the Run-on Sentence	NC1
P-16	P	Conventions	Use Consistent Tense	NC1
P-17	P	Conventions	Use Fragments When You Write a Poem	PC
P-18	P	Final Form	Choose an Appropriate Form	PUBC
P-19	P	Final Form	Choose What Gets Published	PUBC
P-20	P	Final Form	Create Illustrations for the Text	PUBC
P-21	P	Final Form	Reflect on Your Writing	PUBC

† **Key to Cycles:**

LC – Launch Cycle
NC1 – Narrative Cycle 1
NC2 – Narrative Cycle 2
PC – Poetry Cycle
FC – Fiction Cycle
NFC – Nonfiction Cycle
OC1 – Open Cycle 1
OC2 – Open Cycle 2
PubC – Publishing Cycle
TWPC – Test Writing Practice Cycle

Appendix G: Lesson List Arranged by Cycle

Lesson Identifier	Cycle¹	Lesson Title	Quality *=Voice	Sub-Quality
I-1	LC	Create an Authority List	I *	Topics
I-4	LC	Dig Up Buried Stories	I	Topics
I-12	LC	Free-Write for Specifics	I	Details
I-17	LC	Use Supporting Details	I	Details
D-15	LC	Use a Thematic Focus	D *	Focus
D-16	LC	Use a Time Focus	D	Focus
D-30	LC	Find Your Focus	D	Time
L-21	LC	Use Choice Adjectives	L	Word Choice
L-22	LC	Use Precise Nouns	L	Word Choice
L-23	LC	Use Verbs That Describe Action	L	Word Choice
P-8	LC	Be Aware of Words You Commonly Misspell	P	Editing
P-10	LC	Edit with a Checklist	P	Editing
P-11	LC	Fix Spelling Errors	P	Editing
I-8	NC1	Use Plot, Place, and Character in a Story	I	Topics
I-15	NC1	Use General Information and Specific Details	I	Details
I-22	NC1	Bring Your Characters to Life	I*	Character/Setting
I-23	NC1	Describe What Your Characters Look Like	I	Character/Setting
I-24	NC1	Develop the Inner Story	I*	Character/Setting
I-25	NC1	Develop Your Characters	I	Character/Setting
I-27	NC1	Use Details to Bring the Setting Alive	I	Character/Setting
D-3	NC1	Organize Your Writing	D	Organization
D-21	NC1	Write a Lively Lead	D*	Beginnings
D-22	NC1	Write a Waterfall Lead	D	Beginnings
D-23	NC1	Come Up with the Right Ending	D	Endings
D-29	NC1	Develop a Scene	D	Time
L-9	NC1	Use Fresh Language	L	Music
L-13	NC1	Vary Sentence Beginnings	L	Sentences
L-19	NC1	Write Believable Dialogue	L*	Voice
P-5	NC1	Use Parentheses to Add Information	P*	Cool Tools
P-14	NC1	Break a Text into Paragraphs	P	Conventions
P-15	NC1	Stop the Run-on Sentence	P	Conventions
P-16	NC1	Use Consistent Tense	P	Conventions

Lesson Identifier	Cycle¹	Lesson Title	Quality *=Voice	Sub-Quality
I-13	NC2	Invent Specifics to Fill In Memory Gaps	I	Details
I-16	NC2	Use Inference to Let Readers Fill In the Gap	I	Details
D-4	NC2	Use a Recurring Detail	D	Organization
D-7	NC2	Use the 2-3-1 Format for Organization	D	Organization
D-13	NC2	Use a Double Focus in a Narrative	D	Focus
D-24	NC2	End with a Question	D	Endings
D-25	NC2	End with Humor	D*	Endings
D-31	NC2	Use Details to Alter the Pace of Time	D	Time
D-33	NC2	Use a Symmetrical Design	D	Shape
L-1	NC2	Avoid Confusing Pronouns	L	Clarity
L-2	NC2	Avoid Redundant Words	L	Clarity
L-7	NC2	Try Repetition in Narrative Writing	L*	Music
L-12	NC2	Move from Simple to Complex Sentences	L	Sentences
L-17	NC2	Tighten Dialogue	L	Voice
P-1	NC2	Use a Colon to Introduce a List or Idea	P	Cool Tools
P-2	NC2	Use a Semicolon to Pull Together Related Sentences	P	Cool Tools
P-3	NC2	Use Commas to Add an Aside	P	Cool Tools
P-6	NC2	Use the Dash to Spotlight Part of a Sentence	P*	Cool Tools
P-9	NC2	Edit for Passive Voice	P*	Editing
I-2	PC	Create a Poem from a Story	I	Topics
I-3	PC	Create a Poem with Imagery, Emotion, and Music	I	Topics
I-20	PC	Use a Metaphor	I	Compare/Contrast
I-21	PC	Use Personification	I	Compare/Contrast
D-8	PC	Use White Space in a Poem	D	Organization
D-14	PC	Use a Double Focus in a Poem	D	Focus
D-26	PC	End with Your Strongest Line	D	Endings
L-3	PC	Delete the Weak Parts	L	Clarity
L-5	PC	Choose Words That Sound Like What They Mean	L	Music
L-6	PC	Create Line Breaks in a Poem	L	Music
L-8	PC	Use Alliteration	L	Music
L-10	PC	Use Repetition in Poetry	L	Music
L-15	PC	Avoid Clichés	L*	Voice
L-20	PC	Use a Thesaurus to Find Just the Right Word	L	Word Choice
P-17	PC	Use Fragments When You Write a Poem	P	Conventions

Lesson List Arranged by Cycle

Lesson Identifier	Cycle†	Lesson Title	Quality *=Voice	Sub-Quality
I-11	FC	Embellish an Idea	I	Details
I-18	FC	Value Your Experience	I*	Details
I-26	FC	Make Your Story Believable	I	Character/Setting
I-28	FC	Work with an External Conflict	I	Character/Setting
I-29	FC	Work with an Internal Conflict	I*	Character/Setting
I-30	FC	Write in the First Person	I*	Point of View
I-31	FC	Write in the Second Person	I*	Point of View
I-32	FC	Write in the Third Person	I*	Point of View
D-17	FC	Cut to Your Lead	D	Beginnings
D-19	FC	Lead with the Big Picture	D	Beginnings
D-27	FC	Control How Time Moves	D	Time
D-28	FC	Create Suspense in Fiction	D	Time
D-32	FC	Use a Snapshot Structure	D	Shape
D-34	FC	Use a Triangular Structure	D	Shape
D-35	FC	Write a Circular Story or Poem	D	Shape
L-4	FC	Remove Those Annoying Little Qualifiers	L *	Clarity
L-11	FC	Combine Short Sentences	L	Sentences
L-14	FC	Vary the Length of Sentences	L*	Sentences
I-14	NFC	Use Authentic Details	I*	Details
I-19	NFC	Make a Comparison	I	Compare/Contrast
D-1	NFC	Anticipate What the Audience Expects	D	Organization
D-5	NFC	Use a Transition Between Ideas	D	Organization
D-6	NFC	Use Subtitles to Organize Your Writing	D	Organization
D-9	NFC	Capture the Power of One	D*	Focus
D-10	NFC	Find the Right Distance by Pulling in Close	D*	Focus
D-11	NFC	Find the Right Distance by Pulling back	D	Focus
D-18	NFC	Lead with a Question	D*	Beginnings
D-20	NFC	Open with a Scene	D	Beginnings
L-16	NFC	Avoid Passive Verbs	L	Voice
L-18	NFC	Use a Natural Voice	L*	Voice
L-24	NFC	Use Vocabulary Specific to a Subject	L	Word Choice
P-4	NFC	Use Commas to List Ideas	P	Cool Tools
P-7	NFC	Use the Ellipsis	P	Cool Tools

Lesson Identifier	Cycle†	Lesson Title	Quality *=Voice	Sub-Quality
P-12	PUBC	Personalize the Editing Checklist	P	Editing
P-18	PUBC	Choose an Appropriate Form	P	Final Form
P-19	PUBC	Choose What Gets Published	P	Final Form
P-20	PUBC	Create Illustrations for the Text	P	Final Form
P-21	PUBC	Reflect on Your Writing	P	Final Form
I-5	OC1	Find Your Own Purpose for Writing	I	Topics
I-7	OC2	Try a New Genre	I	Topics
I-6	TWPC	Make a Personal Connection	I*	Topics
I-9	TWPC	Use R-U-P-R When Writing to a Prompt	I	Topics
I-10	TWPC	Elaborate on an Idea	I	Details
D-2	TWPC	Include a Beginning, a Middle, and an End	D	Organization
D-12	TWPC	Stay on Topic	D	Focus
P-13	TWPC	Reread for Correctness	P	Editing

† **Key to Cycles:**
LC – Launch Cycle
NC1 – Narrative Cycle 1
NC2 – Narrative Cycle 2
PC – Poetry Cycle
FC – Fiction Cycle
NFC – Nonfiction Cycle
OC1 – Open Cycle 1
OC2 – Open Cycle 2
PubC – Publishing Cycle
TWPC – Test Writing Practice Cycle

Ralph Fletcher
and JoAnn Portalupi

Writing Workshop
THE ESSENTIAL GUIDE

From the authors of *Craft Lessons*

We designed Teaching the Qualities of Writing as a flexible resource that you can adapt to your own unique writing program. We hope you will use TQW in ways that work best for you and your students. While there is no one way to teach writing, our twenty-plus years working with teachers have convinced us that writing workshop, in particular, helps students experience the real pleasures and challenges of writing. If you want to initiate a writing workshop in conjunction with TQW, you'll find that our professional book, ***Writing Workshop: The Essential Guide*** (Heinemann, 2001) provides everything a teacher needs to get the writing workshop up and running. We explain the simple principles that underlie the writing workshop and explore the major components that make it work. Each chapter addresses an essential element, then suggests five or six specific things a teacher can do to implement the idea under discussion. You will also find a separate chapter entitled "What About Skills," which shows how to effectively teach skills in the context of writing. The book closes with practical forms in the appendixes to ensure that the workshop runs smoothly. ***Writing Workshop*** is the culmination of our years of effort, a synthesis of our best thinking on the subject.

You can order ***Writing Workshop: The Essential Guide*** from www.heinemann.com (web orders receive a 10% discount).